ASSESSMENT

PERSONAL AUDIT

	ENTRY LEVEL	ADVANCED LEVEL
SESSION 1 Getting Acquainted	Getting Real Luke 18:9–14	
SESSION 2 Priorities	A Tale of Two Sisters Luke 10:38–42	Eye on the Prize Philippians 3:12–4:1
SESSION 3 Time	Time-out for Moses Exodus 18:13–27	God's Time James 4:13–17; 5:7–8
SESSION 4 Lifestyle	Tough Act to Follow John 13:1–17	Fruit of the Spirit Galatians 5:13–26
SESSION 5 Money	Rich Fool Luke 12:13–21	The Love of Money 1 Timothy 6:3–10,17–19
SESSION 6 Career	Attitudes at Work Matthew 20:1–16	Using Your Gifts Romans 12:1–8
SESSION 7 Future	Walking on Water Matthew 14:22–33	Not to Worry Matthew 6:25–34

Serendipity House / P.O. Box 1012 / Littleton, CO 80160

TOLL FREE 1-800-525-9563 / www.serendipityhouse.com

00 01 / **101 series • CHG** / 4

PROJECT ENGINEER:
Lyman Coleman

WRITING TEAM:
Richard Peace, Lyman Coleman, Matthew Lockhart, Andrew Sloan, Cathy Tardif

PRODUCTION TEAM:
Christopher Werner, Sharon Penington, Erika Tiepel

COVER PHOTO:
© 1998 W. Cody / Westlight

CORE VALUES

Community:	The purpose of this curriculum is to build community within the body of believers around Jesus Christ.
Group Process:	To build community, the curriculum must be designed to take a group through a step-by-step process of sharing your story with one another.
Interactive Bible Study:	To share your "story," the approach to Scripture in the curriculum needs to be open-ended and right brain—to "level the playing field" and encourage everyone to share.
Developmental Stages:	To provide a healthy program in the life cycle of a group, the curriculum needs to offer courses on three levels of commitment: (1) Beginner Stage—low-level entry, high structure, to level the playing field; (2) Growth Stage—deeper Bible study, flexible structure, to encourage group accountability; (3) Discipleship Stage—in-depth Bible study, open structure, to move the group into high gear.
Target Audiences:	To build community throughout the culture of the church, the curriculum needs to be flexible, adaptable and transferable into the structure of the average church.

ACKNOWLEDGMENTS

To Zondervan Bible Publishers
for permission to use
the NIV text,
The Holy Bible, New International Bible Society.
© 1973, 1978, 1984 by International Bible Society.
Used by permission of Zondervan Bible Publishers.

Questions and Answers

PURPOSE

1. What is the purpose of this group?

In a nutshell, the purpose is to get acquainted and to double the size of the group.

STAGE

2. What stage in the life cycle of a small group is this course designed for?

This 101 course is designed for the first stage in the three-stage life cycle of a small group. (See diagram below.) For a full explanation of the three-stage life cycle, see the center section.

GOALS

3. What is the purpose of stage one in the life cycle?

The focus in this first stage is primarily on Group Building.

GROUP BUILDING

4. How does this course develop Group Building?

Take a look at the illustration of the baseball diamond on page M5 in the center section. In the process of using this course, you will go around the four bases.

BIBLE STUDY

5. What is the approach to Bible Study in this course?

As shown on page M4 of the center section, there are two tracks in this book. Track 1 is the light option, based on stories in the Bible. Track 2 is the heavier option, based on teaching passages in the Bible.

THREE-STAGE
LIFE CYCLE
OF A GROUP

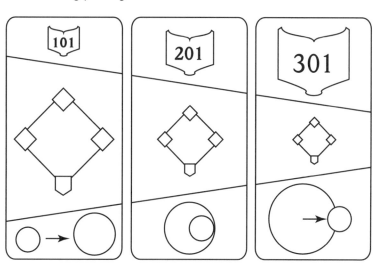

CHOOSING
A TRACK

6. **Which option of Bible Study is best for our group?**

Track 1 is the best option for people not familiar with the Bible as well as for groups who are not familiar with each other. Track 2 is the best option for groups who are familiar with the Bible *and* with one another. (However, whenever you have new people come to a meeting, we recommend you switch to Track 1 for that Bible Study.)

CHOOSING
BOTH OPTIONS

7. **Can we choose both options?**

Yes, depending upon your time schedule. Here's how to decide:

STUDY	APPROXIMATE COMPLETION TIME
Story Sharing only	60–90 minutes
Epistle Study only	60–90 minutes
Story and Epistle Study	90–120 minutes

13-WEEK
PLAN

8. **What if we want to do both the Story and Epistle Studies but don't have time at the session?**

You can spend two weeks on a unit—the Story Questionnaire the first week and the Epistle Study the next. Session 1 has only one Bible Study—so you would end up with 13 weeks if you followed this plan.

BIBLE
KNOWLEDGE

9. **What if you don't know anything about the Bible?**

No problem. The Story option is based on a parable or story that stands on its own—to discuss as though you are hearing it for the first time. The Epistle Study comes with complete reference notes—to help you understand the context of the Bible passage and any difficult words that need to be defined.

THE FEARLESS FOURSOME!

If you have more than seven people at a meeting, Serendipity recommends you divide into groups of 4 for the Bible Study. Count off around the group: "one, two, one, two, etc."—and have the "ones" move quickly to another room for the Bible Study. Ask one person to be the leader and follow the directions for the Bible Study time. After 30 minutes, the Group Leader will call "Time" and ask all groups to come together for the Caring Time.

THE EMPTY
CHAIR

GROUP
COVENANT

GROUND
RULES

10. What is the mission of a 101 group?

Turn to page M5 of the center section. This course is designed for groups in the Birth stage—which means that your mission is to increase the size of the group by filling the "empty chair."

11. How do we fill the empty chair?

Pull up an empty chair during the group's prayer time and ask God to bring a new person to the group to fill it.

12. What is a group covenant?

A group covenant is a "contract" that spells out your expectations and the ground rules for your group. It's very important that your group discuss these issues—preferably as part of the first session.

13. What are the ground rules for the group? (Check those that you agree upon.)

❐ PRIORITY: While you are in the course, you give the group meetings priority.

❐ PARTICIPATION: Everyone participates and no one dominates.

❐ RESPECT: Everyone is given the right to their own opinion and all questions are encouraged and respected.

❐ CONFIDENTIALITY: Anything that is said in the meeting is never repeated outside the meeting.

❐ EMPTY CHAIR: The group stays open to new people at every meeting.

❐ SUPPORT: Permission is given to call upon each other in time of need—even in the middle of the night.

❐ ADVICE GIVING: Unsolicited advice is not allowed.

❐ MISSION: We agree to do everything in our power to start a new group as our mission (see center section).

SESSION

1

Getting Acquainted

3-PART AGENDA

ICE-BREAKER
15 Minutes

BIBLE STUDY
30 Minutes

CARING TIME
15–45 Minutes

Welcome to this course on personal assessment. In this course you will have an opportunity to take an audit of your life in the context of a supportive group.

Our society in the last number of years has been obsessed with the idea of introspection. The self-awareness field extends from scientific analytical personality profiles discovering our colors. Publishers of books and magazines often pri self-discovery inventories, because they know people enjoy taking ther We like to see in black-and-white some measure of who we are and ho we compare to others. Still, many doubt whether the fullness of who w are as individuals can be quantified and registered on a test. Part of th measure of our lives includes the less scientific analysis of how othe see us and respond to us. That is part of what we discover in a group li this one.

> **LEADER:** *Be sure to read the "Questions and Answers" on pages 3–5. Take some time during this first session to have the group go over the ground rules on page 5. At the beginning of the Caring Time have your group look at pages M1–M3 in the center section of this book.*

Self-assessment can be fulfilling experience. But can also be threatenin What happens if we dor like what we find? Th important missing fact for many people is lookir at themselves apart from relationship with God and the values that derive from that relationshi Over the next several weeks we will evaluate our lives in light Scripture. To get the most out of this process, we need to be committe to letting the Word of God challenge us. Honest personal assessment w result in nitty-gritty confrontation between our ways and God's ways. A believers, we can't take assessment of our lives without taking serious Christ's call to discipleship.

In the next several weeks you will have a chance to consider six areas life and to assess yourself in each of these areas:

Priorities	Lifestyle	Career
Time	Money	Future

The Bible study approach in this course is unique, with a little different focus. Usually the content of the Scripture passage is the focus of the Bible Study. In this course, especially in Option 1, the focus will be on telling your spiritual "story" through Scripture.

Every session has three parts: (1) **Ice-Breaker**—to break the ice and introduce the topic, (2) **Bible Study**—to share your life through a passage of Scripture, and (3) **Caring Time**—to share prayer concerns and pray for one another.

Ice-Breaker / 15 Minutes

LEADER: You only have 15 minutes for the Ice-Breaker. Jump on in and get things started by sharing first.

Down Memory Lane. Help your group get to know you better as you celebrate the childhood memories of the way you were. Have each person choose two of the topics listed below and answer the questions related to them. If time allows, do another round.

HOME SWEET HOME: What do you remember about your childhood home?

TELEVISION: What was your favorite TV program?

SCHOOLHOUSE: What were your best and worst subjects in school?

LIBRARY: What did you like to read (and where)?

TELEPHONE: How much time did you spend on the phone each day?

MOVIES: Who was your favorite movie star?

CASH FLOW: What did you do for spending money?

SPORTS: What was your favorite sport or team?

GRANDMA'S HOUSE: Where did your grandparents live? When did you visit them?

POLICE: Did you ever get in trouble with the law?

WEEKENDS: What was the thing to do on Saturday night?

SUMMER VACATION: What family trip do you remember the most?

PETS: What pets did you have growing up?

Bible Study / 30 Minutes

Luke 18:9–14 / Getting Real

This parable that Jesus told is about two very different people. The Pharisee was a member of a strict religious sect within Judaism whose prime concern was keeping the Law of Moses (and other regulations which were added over time). While modern readers assume the Pharisees are the "bad guys," the original audience of this parable respected them as devout, godly men. The tax collector was also a Jew but one who had sold out to the Roman authorities. Jesus' listeners would have considered tax collectors as vile as thieves or murderers. They were seen as traitors, because they collaborated with the Roman power in order to gain wealth (usually dishonestly).

Ask one person to read Luke 18:9–14 out loud. Then discuss the questions with your group. Be sure to save a few minutes at the close to discuss the issues in the Caring Time.

⁹*To some who were confident of their own righteousness and looked down on everybody else, Jesus told this parable:* ¹⁰*"Two men went up to the temple to pray, one a Pharisee and the other a tax collector.* ¹¹*The Pharisee stood up and prayed about himself: 'God, I thank you that I am not like other men—robbers, evildoers, adulterers—or even like this tax collector.* ¹²*I fast twice a week and give a tenth of all I get.'*

¹³*"But the tax collector stood at a distance. He would not even look up to heaven, but beat his breast and said, 'God, have mercy on me, a sinner.'*

¹⁴*"I tell you that this man, rather than the other, went home justified before God. For everyone who exalts himself will be humbled, and he who humbles himself will be exalted."*

1. How do you feel about the Pharisee in this story?
   ❐ I feel sorry for him.
   ❐ I feel a little angry.
   ❐ I feel like punching him out.
   ❐ I have the same attitude that he does.

2. Why do you think the Pharisee acted like he did?
   ❐ He was grateful to God and wanted to honor him.
   ❐ He was arrogantly self-righteous.
   ❐ He was influenced by peer pressure.
   ❐ He wouldn't be real with others.
   ❐ He wouldn't be real with himself.

3. How do you feel about the tax collector?
- ❐ At least he's honest.
- ❐ I can relate to this guy.
- ❐ After cheating people, he has some nerve!
- ❐ I think he was being just as phony as the Pharisee.
- ❐ It depends on whether he changed his ways when he got home.

4. Why do you think the tax collector acted like he did?
- ❐ He knew he had done wrong.
- ❐ He wanted sympathy.
- ❐ He had a poor self-image.
- ❐ He was plea-bargaining with God.
- ❐ He had hit rock bottom.

5. How much of the Pharisee and the tax collector do you see in yourself? Put a percentage for each—and the two must add up to 100%.

I see myself as _____% Pharisee and _____% tax collector.

6. From what area of your life do you derive your greatest self-confidence?
- ❐ my job / career
- ❐ my athletic ability / physical condition
- ❐ my marriage
- ❐ my money / material assets
- ❐ my parenting
- ❐ my friendships
- ❐ my spiritual life
- ❐ my accomplishments
- ❐ my intelligence
- ❐ other:_____
- ❐ my education / degrees

7. In all honesty, how do you view yourself right now? Put an *"X"* on the lines below:

I make excuses for my faults. _____I take responsibility for my faults.

I always put myself down._____I see myself like God does.

People reject me. _____People accept me.

God rejects me. _____God accepts me.

8. With whom do you "get real" and share your life, including your problems?
- ❐ my spouse
- ❐ my boyfriend or girlfriend
- ❐ my parents
- ❐ this group
- ❐ another family member
- ❐ no one
- ❐ a close friend
- ❐ other:_____
- ❐ my pastor

"God knows, I'm not the thing I should be, nor am I even the thing I could be."
—Robert Burns

9

9. How do you feel about taking an "audit" of your life through this course and sharing personal matters with this group?

❏ uncomfortable—I don't talk about these things.

❏ scared—I don't know if I want to talk about these things.

❏ okay—I can handle it.

❏ happy—I know I need this kind of sharing.

❏ thrilled—I love this stuff!

❏ I'm not sure.

❏ other:_____

Caring Time / 15–45 Minutes

LEADER:
Ask the group, "Who are you going to invite next week?"

The most important time in every meeting is this—Caring Time—where you take time to share prayer requests and pray for one another. To make sure that this time is not neglected, you need to set a minimum time that you will devote to prayer requests and prayer and count backwards from the closing time by this amount. For instance, if you are going to close at 9 p.m., and you are going to devote 30 minutes to prayer requests and prayer, you need to ask a timekeeper to call "time" at 8:30 and move to prayer requests. Start out by asking everyone to answer the question:

"How can we help you in prayer this week?"

Then, move into prayer. If you have not prayed out loud before, finish these sentences:

"Hello, God, this is ... (first name). I want to thank you for ..."

GROUP DIRECTORY

P.S.
At the close, pass around your books and have everyone sign the Group Directory inside the front cover.

SESSION

2

Priorities

3-PART AGENDA

ICE-BREAKER
15 Minutes

BIBLE STUDY
30 Minutes

CARING TIME
15–45 Minutes

A logical place to begin a personal assessment is in the area of priorities. Someone has said, concerning personal goals, that if you aim at nothing you will hit it every time. In taking an audit of our lives, we need to begin by asking ourselves what we are aiming at. What is most important to us? What will it take to get there? What do we need to change to be consistent with our goals and priorities?

When it comes to setting goals and priorities, it's easy to fall into extremes. On one hand, it's tempting for us to have a *que sera sera* approach to life. We simply want to take each day as it comes and not beat ourselves up with a bunch of unmet expectations for our behavior. The problem here is that we know internally that God has placed in us the motivation to meet a set of standards in our lives.

The other extreme we can fall into is a legalistic approach to life. Whether we are driven by religious obligation or our own perfectionism, we never seem to meet our inner expectations—and thus deal with frustration and guilt. For some, the compulsion to set personal goals is so intense that they cannot live in the present or really feel satisfied when they do achieve their goals.

LEADER: *If there are new people in this session, review the ground rules for this group on page 5. Have the group look at page M4 in the center section and decide which Bible Study option to use—light or heavy. If you have more than seven people, see the box about the "Fearless Foursome" on page 4.*

The biblical approach lies balanced between these two extremes. We know that God has a plan for our lives, both in terms of the big picture of what we are called to do and in principles for how we should live our lives on a daily basis. However, we also know that it is only by God's grace that we can fulfill these responsibilities. And, in fact, as long as we are on this earth we will fall short of God's standards. Nonetheless, God has made us with the capacity and drive to set goals and priorities. He has given us the Holy Spirit to enable us to live out those priorities, both for our good and God's glory. And along the way God wants us to enjoy the journey—seeing each day as an opportunity and a gift.

In this session, we will consider proper priorities. In the Option 1 Study (from the Gospel of Luke), we will look at a story where Jesus points out to two sisters what really matters in life. In the Option 2 Study (from the apostle Paul's letter to the Philippians), we will observe Paul's driving force in life.

This session builds on the last session which emphasized the importance of "getting real" with God, ourselves and other people. An important part of this course is doing personal assessment as part of a relationship with this group. Be sure to save plenty of time in this session for the Caring Time—to share your concerns and pray for one another. This is what the course is all about.

Ice-Breaker / 15 Minutes

Mutual Funds. You have each just been given $10,000 to invest in various mutual funds. Looking at one fund at a time, have the group share how much they want to invest in each fund.

_____ AGGRESSIVE CHRISTIAN GROWTH FUND: This fund will give great returns to help you grow in your faith. The dividends include a greater love for God and a deeper commitment to your church.

_____ FIDELITY MARRIAGE FUND: This fund will help to ensure that your marriage is a wonderful and loving relationship. The prospectus promises great communication and a joyful family life.

_____ BALANCED TIME FUND: This fund will help you to budget your time effectively so your life is balanced. The broker says that this fund is a favorite of people who say they are too busy.

_____ CONSERVATIVE VALUES FUND: This fund will help your family return to the homegrown, traditional lifestyle of your ancestors. This fund includes such stocks as Honest Industries, Hard Work Mining and Family Products.

_____ FRIENDSHIP BOND FUND: The payoff of this fund is closer and deeper friendships. It boasts timeless dividends and wealth that "cannot be measured."

_____ CARIBBEAN RESTORATION FUND: This fund will take you to exotic places for rest and relaxation. This is a good fund for someone who needs to spend a little on themselves.

_____ SECURITY RAINY DAY FUND: This mutual fund promises to pay dividends for a rainy day. It is a safe hedge against any problem or disaster, and will keep you from worrying about unexpected problems.

_____ INTELLIGENT STRENGTH FUND: This is a fund which is especially designed for people who need to save money for college. Money invested in this fund will be ready to help a prospective student pay for tuition.

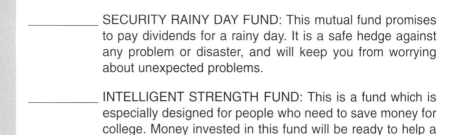

Bible Study / 30 Minutes

Option 1 / Gospel Study

Luke 10:38–42 / A Tale of Two Sisters

In this story, Jesus visits the home of his friends, Martha and Mary, and helps them set right priorities. Have someone read Luke 10:38–42 out loud, and then discuss your responses to the following questions with your group.

³⁸As Jesus and his disciples were on their way, he came to a village where a woman named Martha opened her home to him. ³⁹She had a sister called Mary, who sat at the Lord's feet listening to what he said. ⁴⁰But Martha was distracted by all the preparations that had to be made. She came to him and asked, "Lord, don't you care that my sister has left me to do the work by myself? Tell her to help me!"

⁴¹"Martha, Martha," the Lord answered, "you are worried and upset about many things, ⁴²but only one thing is needed. Mary has chosen what is better, and it will not be taken away from her."

1. Why do you think Martha drove herself like she did in this story?
  ❑ She wasn't into small groups and Bible studies.
  ❑ She was a Type A personality—drive, drive, drive.
  ❑ She wanted to impress Jesus.
  ❑ She had the gift of serving.
  ❑ She wanted to make herself look better than her sister Mary.
  ❑ She loved Jesus.

2. Why do you think Mary was sitting at Jesus' feet?
   - ❐ She wanted to be ready to wait on Jesus.
   - ❐ She wasn't aware of the work that needed to be done.
   - ❐ She was a "people person."
   - ❐ She wanted to learn all she could.
   - ❐ She was lazy and didn't want to help her sister Martha.
   - ❐ She loved Jesus.

3. Comparing yourself to these two sisters, which of them are you more like?
   - ❐ Martha—responsible and uptight
   - ❐ Mary—carefree and laid-back

4. If you were Martha, how would you have responded to Jesus' remark?
   - ❐ gone to my room and pouted
   - ❐ thought to myself: "He doesn't have to live with my sister."
   - ❐ flown off the handle
   - ❐ explained why I needed Mary's help
   - ❐ accepted the correction, sat down with Mary, and let supper burn

5. What was Jesus saying to Martha?
   - ❐ She should chill out.
   - ❐ She should be more like Mary.
   - ❐ She had her priorities messed up.
   - ❐ Work isn't important.
   - ❐ People are more important than work.
   - ❐ "Sitting at Jesus' feet" is more important than anything else.

6. If Jesus stopped by *your* house and observed you in action, what would be his advice to you?
   - ❐ "Turn down the noise and be quiet."
   - ❐ "Get focused—figure out what you need to do and do it."
   - ❐ "Set aside more time to spend with me."
   - ❐ "Don't worry about the things you can't do anything about."
   - ❐ "Slow down—you're always in a hurry."
   - ❐ "Be a little more sensitive to the other members of your family."
   - ❐ "Look after your spiritual life like you do your body."
   - ❐ other:_____

7. In what area of your life do you need to work at changing your priorities?
   - ❐ my spiritual life
   - ❐ my family life
   - ❐ my vocational life
   - ❐ my leisure life
   - ❐ my physical lifestyle and habits
   - ❐ other:_____

8. What "one thing is needed" for you to set right priorities in your life?
   ❏ I need to find a "Martha" to do all my work for me.
   ❏ I need to adopt Mary's relaxed, reflective style.
   ❏ I need to learn more about Jesus and what he thinks is important in life.
   ❏ I need to be closer to Jesus personally.
   ❏ other:_____

9. How could others in your group or church help you in this?
   ❏ by helping me understand what is going on inside of me
   ❏ by leaving me alone
   ❏ by telling me it's okay to be me
   ❏ by sharing some of their own struggles
   ❏ by challenging me to be all that I can be
   ❏ other:_____

Option 2 / Epistle Study

Philippians 3:12–4:1 / Eye on the Prize

LEADER: Remember— for the Option 2 / Epistle Study there are Reference Notes for the passage.

In his letter to the Philippians, the apostle Paul has just written of his quest "to know Christ and the power of his resurrection and the fellowship of sharing in his sufferings, becoming like him ..." Now he states that while spiritual perfection is not attainable in this life we should be motivated by such a goal. Read Philippians 3:12–4:1 and discuss the questions with your group.

¹²Not that I have already obtained all this, or have already been made perfect, but I press on to take hold of that for which Christ Jesus took hold of me. ¹³Brothers, I do not consider myself yet to have taken hold of it. But one thing I do: Forgetting what is behind and straining toward what is ahead, ¹⁴I press on toward the goal to win the prize for which God has called me heavenward in Christ Jesus.

¹⁵All of us who are mature should take such a view of things. And if on some point you think differently, that too God will make clear to you. ¹⁶Only let us live up to what we have already attained.

¹⁷Join with others in following my example, brothers, and take note of those who live according to the pattern we gave you. ¹⁸For, as I have often told you before and now say again even with tears, many live as enemies of the cross of Christ. ¹⁹Their destiny is destruction, their god is their stomach, and their glory is in their shame. Their mind is on earthly things. ²⁰But our citizenship is in heaven. And we eagerly await a Savior from there, the Lord Jesus Christ, ²¹who, by the power that enables him to bring everything

Scripture continued on page 16

under his control, will transform our lowly bodies so that they will be lik *his glorious body.*

4 *Therefore, my brothers, you whom I love and long for, my joy an crown, that is how you should stand firm in the Lord, dear friends!*

1. What past award or accomplishment (in sports, music, school, wor etc.) do you value the most?

2. What goal have you recently achieved? What goal is still in process

3. Using the imagery of a track race, where does Paul picture himself his spiritual life? What prize is he after (see notes on 3:14)?

4. What are you passionate about? In what area of your life do yo strive the most for excellence?

5. Why is it necessary to forget the past and look to the future in o Christian lives? When it comes to moving on and letting go of th past, what grade would you give yourself?

6. If a person isn't sure what proper priorities in life should be, wh does Paul advise (3:17)? Who do you look up to as a model for yo life?

7. What kind of balance is there in your life between "earthly things" ar spiritual or "heavenly" things (3:19–20)?

8. If you compared your Christian life to a track race, where would yo be right now: Sitting on the sidelines? Warming up? At the startir block? Giving it your all? Gutting it out? Giving up?

9. What change in priorities do you need in order to "press on towa the goal" which God has called you? How can this group hold ye accountable for that?

Caring Time / 15–45 Minutes

LEADER:
Ask the group, "Who are you going to invite next week?"

In the Option 1 Scripture, Jesus said that Martha was "worried and upset about many things." Share personal prayer requests by answering the question:

"What are you most worried or upset about right now?"

Then go around and let each person pray for the person on their right. Start with this sentence:

"Dear God, I want to speak to you about my friend _____."

During your prayer time, remember to pray for the empty chair and for the growth of your group.

Reference Notes

Summary. In the previous passage, Paul laid bare his heart to the Philippians. He described how in contrast to his former reliance on an impeccable heritage and on zealous striving to obey the Law, now his driving passion had become that of "knowing Christ." This is what motivated him. This is what consumed him. In this passage, he describes in more detail what it means to strive to take hold of Christ. Here he also warns against anyone who might feel that they have already "arrived" spiritually and thus attained "perfection." Over against this pattern of striving to know Christ (vv. 12–14) which he enjoins the Philippians to follow (vv. 15–17), Paul sets the pattern modeled by the false teachers (vv. 18–19). Their concern is with food laws and circumcision—"earthly things"—in contrast to the heavenly kingdom to which Christians belong.

3:12 *Not that.* Paul disclaims that he has reached any sort of perfection in his spiritual life, or has fully comprehended who Christ is.

obtained. This is a difficult word to translate because it has such a wide range of meanings. It can be translated "to take hold of," "to apprehend," "to comprehend," as well as "to obtain." It probably refers to comprehending fully on a mental and spiritual level just who Jesus Christ is.

perfect. This is the only time in his epistles that Paul uses this word. He borrows it (probably) from the vocabulary of the mystery religions. They offered to devotees the "secret" that would enable them to attain a sort of blissful perfection which would end their earthly struggles. In contrast, Paul indicates that he has not yet fully understood Jesus Christ. There is simply too much to know of Christ ever to grasp it all this side of heaven. Thus the Jewish teachers are wrong when they say that if people are circumcised and keep the Law, they can attain perfection.

press on. In contrast to those groups that claim it is possible to attain spiritual perfection here and now, the Christian life is one of relentless striving to know Christ in his fullness.

to take hold of. This is another difficult word to translate. It can refer to winning a prize, as for example, in a race. Or it can mean to understand or comprehend something.

Jesus took hold of me. Paul refers here to his conversion experience on the Damascus Road.

3:13 consider. This word means "to calculate precisely." Paul means that after looking carefully at his life and all he has experienced of Christ, he has come to the conclusion that he has a long way to go in his spiritual pilgrimage.

Forgetting what is behind. In order to press on to a successful conclusion of his spiritual pilgrimage, Paul must first cease looking at his past. He must forget past failures (such as persecuting the church). He must also forget past successes (such as reaching the pinnacle of Jewish spirituality). Neither guilt nor personal attainment will assist him in gaining Christ.

what is ahead. If the first movement in the spiritual pilgrimage is to forget the past, the second movement is to concentrate totally on what lies ahead—full comprehension of Jesus Christ. Christians are urged forward by what the future holds instead of simply running away from what they did in their past.

3:14 goal. This is the mark on the track that signifies the end of the race.

the prize. What Paul seems to have in mind is the moment at the end of the race, when the winner is called forward by the games master to receive the victory palm or wreath. Likewise, on the day of resurrection the Christian will be called forward by God to receive the prize, which is full knowledge of Christ Jesus.

3:15–16 Although some in Philippi consider themselves to have arrived at spiritual perfection, Paul knows this is not possible. He also knows that such folk view this matter differently than he, and that they will not be convinced by what he says. Paul is confident that God will in time reveal the truth to them. In the meantime, he encourages them not to let these differences in understanding impede growth and harmony in the church.

3:15 *mature.* This is the same word that is translated "perfect" in verse 12. He uses this word in a slightly ironic way here: "Those of us who might think we are 'perfect' know that there is no such thing as true perfection. There is only continual striving to comprehend Christ."

3:17 *the pattern.* Paul has defined the pattern for the Christian life as forgetting what is behind and constantly forging ahead to grasp the fullness of Jesus Christ on all levels of one's being.

3:18 *with tears.* These are tears of frustration on Paul's part, that his beloved countrymen continue to reject the Gospel.

enemies of the cross. It was the fact of Jesus' death that so scandalized the Jews. They found it almost impossible to accept that God could will and work through a crucified Messiah.

3:19 *their god is their stomach.* The Jews were obsessed with laws relating to what they could eat and drink, how and when to eat, ritual preparation for eating, etc. A key feature of their religious life thus involved the issue of food.

shame. Probably refers to nakedness, and thus this is a reference to circumcision (which was another key feature of the Jewish religious life). In other words, food laws and circumcision had become gods to these people (Hawthorne).

3:20 *eagerly await.* Paul captures the keen anticipation and happy expectation of the Christians who long for Christ's return, at which time they will be rescued from their trials and will experience new life in all its fullness.

4:1 *crown.* This is the wreath of wild olive leaves laced with parsley and bay leaves that was awarded to the victor in athletic competition.

GROUP DIRECTORY

P.S.
If you have a new person in your group, be sure to add their name to the group directory inside the front cover.

Time

3-PART AGENDA

ICE-BREAKER
15 Minutes

BIBLE STUDY
30 Minutes

CARING TIME
15–45 Minutes

Time is that mystical commodity we all possess equally and for which most of us long to have more. Many of us have paid large amounts of money to attend time management seminars or purchase time management resources. (Others of us have been interested in taking advantage of such opportunities, but haven't had the time!)

Taking a personal audit of our lives wouldn't be complete without focusing on how we use our time. In the last session, we considered our priorities. The next step is to apply those priorities to where the rubber hits the road—in the use of our time. If there's any doubt about how much we value time, consider some of the many phrases in our vocabulary concerning time. We can make time, keep time, lose time, or gain time; we can be on time, ahead of time, behind time, or out of time!

LEADER: If there are more than seven people at this meeting, divide into groups of 4 for the Bible Study. Count off around the group: "one, two, one, two, etc."—and have the "ones" quickly move to another room. When you come back together for the Caring Time, have the group read about your Mission on page M5 of the center section.

Some churches ask their members to commit themselves to give of their "talents, treasures and time." We may be the most sensitive about giving of money or being told how to manage our finances. But chances are that we are even more protective of our time. Of course, as with everything else in life, when we take Christian principles seriously, we realize that our time is at God's disposal. This thing we call time is a gift from God, and how we spend it is a direct reflection of how we perceive God and our faith.

In the Option 1 Bible story from the Old Testament, we see Moses in a situation where his time was consumed by the needs of others. In the Option 2 Study (from the book of James), we will consider what perspective we should have about using our time and planning ahead.

Ice-Breaker / 15 Minutes

Precious Time. God has given us a precious gift: the time to live. Maybe that's why now is called "the present." Taking one at a time, complete the following three sentences about precious time—sharing your answers with your group.

MY IDEA OF A GREAT TIME IS ...

❒ a quiet evening at home
❒ watching a good movie
❒ a hot bath after a long day
❒ reading a good book
❒ a brisk walk on a fall afternoon
❒ a day shopping with friends
❒ hard work that pays off
❒ watching an exciting sports event
❒ playing my favorite game or sport
❒ a night out
❒ fishing or hiking
❒ going to a party
❒ a delicious meal
❒ going to a great concert
❒ other:_____

WHAT MAKES A BAD DAY FOR ME IS ...

❒ crummy weather
❒ mood swings
❒ boring work or classes
❒ conflict with others
❒ being alone on a weekend
❒ lousy financial news
❒ Mondays
❒ paying bills
❒ heavy traffic
❒ my team losing
❒ other:_____

IF I HAD ONLY THREE MONTHS TO LIVE, I WOULD SPEND MY TIME ...

❒ seeing the world
❒ writing my memoirs
❒ finishing my "big project"
❒ spending all my money
❒ giving everything away
❒ climbing Mt. Everest
❒ doing all I could for God
❒ being with friends and family
❒ doing exactly what I'm doing now
❒ partying
❒ being very angry
❒ loving everyone more
❒ other:_____

Bible Study / 30 Minutes

Option 1 / Story Passage

Exodus 18:13–27 / Time-out for Moses

Not long before this story took place, God had miraculously delivered the Israelites from slavery in Egypt. Moses, God's specially chosen leader, was now directing this throng of people through the wilderness toward the promised land. Moses was working extremely hard to teach the people God's ways. One means by which he did this was by judging their disputes. Moses' father-in-law, Jethro, has just come to visit the Israelite camp. Have someone read Exodus 18:13–27 and then discuss the questions with your group.

¹³The next day Moses took his seat to serve as judge for the people, and they stood around him from morning till evening. ¹⁴When his father-in-law saw all that Moses was doing for the people, he said, "What is this you are doing for the people? Why do you alone sit as judge, while all these people stand around you from morning till evening?"

¹⁵Moses answered him, "Because the people come to me to seek God's will. ¹⁶Whenever they have a dispute, it is brought to me, and I decide between the parties and inform them of God's decrees and laws."

¹⁷Moses' father-in-law replied, "What you are doing is not good. ¹⁸You and these people who come to you will only wear yourselves out. The work is too heavy for you; you cannot handle it alone. ¹⁹Listen now to me and I will give you some advice, and may God be with you. You must be the people's representative before God and bring their disputes to him. ²⁰Teach them the decrees and laws, and show them the way to live and the duties they are to perform. ²¹But select capable men from all the people—men who fear God, trustworthy men who have dishonest gain—and appoint them as officials over thousands, hundreds, fifties and tens. ²²Have them serve as judges for the people at all times, but have them bring every difficult case to you; the simple cases they can decide themselves. That will make your load lighter, because they will share it with you. ²³If you do this and God so commands, you will be able to stand the strain, and all these people will go home satisfied."

²⁴Moses listened to his father-in-law and did everything he said. ²⁵He chose capable men from all Israel and made them leaders of the people, officials over thousands, hundreds, fifties and tens. ²⁶They served as judges for the people at all times. The difficult cases they brought to Moses, but the simple ones they decided themselves.

²⁷Then Moses sent his father-in-law on his way, and Jethro returned to his own country.

1. If you were Moses, how would you have felt about your father-in-law's advice?
   - ❏ scolded
   - ❏ excited
   - ❏ cared for
   - ❏ threatened
   - ❏ skeptical
   - ❏ relieved

2. Why do you think Moses worked so hard?
   - ❏ He was a workaholic.
   - ❏ He was a perfectionist.
   - ❏ He hated to say no.
   - ❏ He liked to be in control.
   - ❏ He felt that no one else could do what he was doing.
   - ❏ He had a need to please others.
   - ❏ He thought he was doing what God wanted.
   - ❏ A creative solution hadn't been suggested.

3. To the extent you work too hard at something, what is the reason?
   - ❏ I am a workaholic.
   - ❏ I am a perfectionist.
   - ❏ I hate to say no.
   - ❏ I like to be in control.
   - ❏ I have a need to please others.
   - ❏ I feel like no one else can do what I am doing.
   - ❏ I am doing what I think God wants.
   - ❏ A creative solution hasn't been suggested.

4. Judging by what you do with your discretionary time, what award or honor are you seeking?
   - ❏ "Parent of the Year" (popularity with my kids)
   - ❏ "Grandparent of the Year" (popularity with my grandkids)
   - ❏ "Employee of the Month" ... every month (earning respect at work)
   - ❏ "Fan of the Year" (awarded by my favorite team or celebrity)
   - ❏ Honorary degree in _____ (for academic achievement)
   - ❏ "Volunteer of the Year" (satisfying my need to be needed)
   - ❏ "Alumni of the Year" (for outstanding service to my alma mater)
   - ❏ "_____'s Hall of Fame" (for sports achievement)
   - ❏ President of _____ (earning respect of colleagues)
   - ❏ Oscar, Emmy or Grammy award for acting or musical ability
   - ❏ Winner of the Nobel Prize in _____ (for my efforts in the cause I have dedicated myself to)
   - ❏ other:_____

5. Which of the following would be a strength in your life? Which would be a weakness?
❐ settling other people's disputes
❐ listening to suggestions
❐ giving constructive criticism
❐ accepting criticism
❐ delegating responsibility
❐ managing my time
❐ saying no to requests

6. In which area listed in the previous question do you most want change? What is one thing you can do to grow in that area?

7. What responsibility has been wearing you out lately?
❐ taking care of the kids
❐ bringing home the bacon
❐ taking care of a parent
❐ dealing with demands at work
❐ settling family disputes
❐ carrying out church commitments
❐ not any one responsibility—but juggling them all
❐ other:_____

8. Where do you sense God challenging you to spend more time?
❐ in prayer and personal Bible study
❐ in my work or in career enhancement
❐ in church activities
❐ with my family
❐ in physical exercise
❐ in resting or sleeping
❐ in personal renewal through leisure activities
❐ other:_____

9. In order to make time for the answer you gave to the last question (as well as for any other reason), where do you sense God challenging you to spend *less* time?

James 4:13–17; 5:7–8 / God's Time

The epistle of James is known for its direct, even blunt, exhortations about living out the Christian faith. In 4:13–17, James is specifically addressing Christian merchants about their attitude toward their time and their future. These excerpts from James' letter challenge our perspective about time as well. Read the Scripture and discuss the questions which follow with your group.

¹³Now listen, you who say, "Today or tomorrow we will go to this or that city, spend a year there, carry on business and make money." ¹⁴Why, you do not even know what will happen tomorrow. What is your life? You are a mist that appears for a little while and then vanishes. ¹⁵Instead, you ought to say, "If it is the Lord's will, we will live and do this or that." ¹⁶As it is, you boast and brag. All such boasting is evil. ¹⁷Anyone, then, who knows the good he ought to do and doesn't do it, sins. ...

⁷Be patient, then, brothers, until the Lord's coming. See how the farmer waits for the land to yield its valuable crop and how patient he is for the autumn and spring rains. ⁸You too, be patient and stand firm, because the Lord's coming is near.

1. When you were 14, what did you expect to be doing at age 24? How close were you to being right?

2. How would James' words go over today in a speech at a convention of business owners? How would you feel if some preacher got on your case about how you spent time and made plans in your business?

> *"Life is a little gleam of time between two eternities."*
> —Thomas Carlyle

3. In contrast to the arrogant statement made by the merchants in 4:13, how should a Christian think (see notes on 4:15)?

4. How often is your outlook like that which James calls for in 4:14–15? Would you say you have the proper balance between planning ahead and living one day at a time?

5. What does 4:17 say about the way Christians should use their time?

6. Take a moment to reflect on how 4:17 is true in your life. What situa tion comes to mind, and what is usually the reason you don't tak time to do what you know you should?

"I fail or succeed in my stewardship of life in proportion to how convinced I am that life belongs to God."
—Pearl Bartel

7. What does James challenge his readers to do in 5:7–8? Do you cor sider yourself a patient person?

8. On a scale of 1 (not at all) to 10 (totally), to what extent does you commitment to God affect how you spend your time? How you view your future?

9. What's something in your life which you've been waiting for a lon time? How are you doing on being patient and standing firm in you faith (5:8)?

Caring Time / 15–45 Minutes

Take some time to share any personal prayer requests ar answer the question:

"How do you need God's help in any struggles you're having with setting priorities or using time?"

LEADER:
Ask the group, "Who are you going to invite next week?"

Close with a short time of prayer, remembering the requests that hav been shared. If you would like to pray in silence, say the word "Ame when you have finished your prayer, so that the next person will kno when to start.

Summary. James begins discussion of his third and final theme: testing. He will deal with this theme, at first, as it touches the issue of wealth. The problem is the difficulty that comes from being wealthy and the tensions this brings, both on a personal level and for the whole community. In this first part of his discussion (4:13–17), he looks at the situation of a group of Christian businessmen—in particular, at their "sins of omission."

4:13 Boasting about what will happen tomorrow is another example of human arrogance. It is arrogant because God is the only one who knows what will happen in the future.

Now listen. This is literally "Come now." It stands in sharp contrast to the way James has been addressing his readers. In the previous section he called them "my brother" (3:1,12). James reverts to this more impersonal language in addressing these merchants.

"Today or tomorrow we will go ..." James lets us listen in on the plans of a group of businessmen. Possibly they are looking at a map together. In any case, they are planning for the future and are concerned with where they will go, how long they will stay, what they will do, and how much profit they will make. It appears to be an innocent conversation. "In trade a person has to plan ahead: Travel plans, market projections, time frames, profit forecasts are the stuff of business in all ages. Every honest merchant would plan in exactly the same way—pagan, Jew or Christian—and that is exactly the problem James has with these plans: There is absolutely nothing about their desires for the future, their use of money, or their way of doing business that is any different from the rest of the world. Their worship may be exemplary, their personal morality, impeccable; but when it comes to business they think entirely on a world-ly plane" (Davids, GNC).

4:14 ***tomorrow.*** All such planning presupposes that tomorrow will unfold like any other day, when in fact the future is anything but secure (see Prov. 27:1).

What is your life? Is it not death that is the great unknown? Who can know when death will come and interrupt plans? "Their projections are made; their plans are laid. But it all hinges on a will higher than theirs, a God unconsulted in their planning. That very night disease might strike; suddenly their plans evaporate, their only trip being one on a bier to a cold grave. ... By thinking on the worldly plane, James' Christian business people have gained a false sense of security. They need to look death in the face and realize their lack of control over life" (Davids, GNC).

mist. Hosea 13:3 says, "Therefore they will be like the morning mist, like the early dew that disappears, like chaff swirling from a threshing floor, like smoke escaping through a window."

● **4:15** *"If it is the Lord's will."* This phrase (often abbreviated D.V. after its Latin form) is not used in the Old Testament, though it was found frequently in Greek and Roman literature and is used by Paul (see Ac 18:21; 1 Cor. 4:19; 16:7). The uncertainty of the future ought not to be a terror to the Christian. Instead, it ought to force on him or her an awareness of how dependent a person is upon God, and thus move that person to planning that involves God.

we will live and do this or that. James is not ruling out planning. He says plan, but keep God in mind.

4:16 In contrast to such prayerful planning, these Christian merchants are very proud of what they do on their own. James is not condemning international trade as such, nor the wealth it produced. (His comments on riches come in 5:1–3.) What he is concerned about is that all this is done without reference to God, in a spirit of boastful arrogance.

boast. The problem with this boasting is that they are claiming to have the future under control when, in fact, it is God who holds time in his hands. These are empty claims.

brag. This word originally described an itinerant quack who touted "cures" that did not work. It came to mean claiming to be able to do something you could not do.

4:17 Some feel that this proverb-like statement may, in fact, be a saying of Jesus that did not get recorded in the Gospel accounts. In any case, by it James points out the nature of so-called "sins of omission." In other words, it is sin when we fail to do what we ought to do. The more familiar definition is of "sins of commission" or wrongdoing (see 1 John 3:4). In other words, sinning can be both active and passive. Christians can sin by doing what they ought not to do (law-breaking); or by not doing what they know they should do (failure).

5:7–8 James begins this concluding section by summarizing his ideas about testing.

5:7 patient. This word carries with it the idea of "self-restraint in the face of injustice." The opposite response would be retaliation or vengeance (see Rom. 2:4 and 1 Peter 3:20).

brothers. James has shifted back into this personal form of address (as in 4:11 and elsewhere), away from his impersonal tone in 4:13 and 5:1. The whole atmosphere of the passage has changed from that of warning and command (in 4:13–5:6) to encouragement and gentle instruction.

28

Lifestyle

3-PART AGENDA

ICE-BREAKER
15 Minutes

BIBLE STUDY
30 Minutes

CARING TIME
15–45 Minutes

All Christians, by definition, are nonconformists. By choice, they are out of step with secular culture. They see reality through a different lens than those around them. This leads to a lifestyle that may seem unconventional. As a result, they bring new light to the society around them. However, the danger Christians face is that of being sucked back into the norms of their culture (which the Bible calls "the world"—by which it means the anti-God principle that infects all cultural systems).

Jesus ushered in the kingdom of God. But this kingdom is very different than what one would expect. It has aptly been called the "upside-down kingdom," since prevailing assumptions about kings and dominions have been reversed. One of the marks of the citizens of God's kingdom is a lifestyle of service. Jesus came as a servant and calls his followers, while not ignoring their own needs, to do likewise.

> **LEADER: If you have a new person at this session, remember to use Option 1 rather than Option 2 for the Bible Study. During the Caring Time, don't forget to keep praying for the empty chair.**

The Bible story in the Option 1 Study is probably the classic instance of Jesus' demonstration of servanthood: the occasion of Jesus the master washing his disciples' feet. In the Option 2 Study (from the letter to the Galatians), the apostle Paul echoes this theme of serving one another. He goes on to elaborate on a lifestyle of love: it is a lifestyle that conforms to the Spirit of God rather than to the desires of the sinful nature.

After doing the following Ice-Breaker and the Bible Study, remember to save plenty of time for the Caring Time—to share your concerns and pray for one another.

Ice-Breaker / 15 Minutes

Life Signs. Think about your lives in terms of traffic signs. Takin[g] one question at a time, have each person share their responses.

1. If you were to select a traffic sign to tell how you've been seeking [to] live your life, what sign would it be?
   - ❑ "Merge"—because I've been trying to get along with everyone
   - ❑ "Slow"—because I've been seeking to slow down and experienc[e] more of life
   - ❑ "Keep Right"—because I'm trying to keep my life on the right trac[k]
   - ❑ "No U-Turn"—because I'm resisting the urge to go back to the pa[st]
   - ❑ "One Way"—because I'm seeking to be more decisive in my life
   - ❑ "Yield"—because I'm seeking to yield my life to God
   - ❑ "Children Playing"—because I'm trying to let out the "child" in me
   - ❑ "Under Construction"—because I'm changing so much

2. What signs are you displaying in your relationship with others?
   - ❑ "No Trespassing!"—because I keep people at a distance
   - ❑ "Help Wanted"—because I'm reaching out for support
   - ❑ "One Way"—because I'm not always tolerant of differences
   - ❑ "Open 24 Hours"—because I'm always available to others
   - ❑ "Keep Right"—because I encourage others to do what is right
   - ❑ "No Vacancy"—because there's no room in my life for anyone el[se] right now

3. If God were to give you a "traffic ticket" right now for how you are l[iv]ing your life, what would it be for?
   - ❑ "Speeding"—not slowing down enough to really live
   - ❑ "Failing to Yield"—trying to do things my own way
   - ❑ "Blocking Traffic"—I feel I've gotten in the way of others who a[re] doing more.
   - ❑ "Illegal U-Turn"—I have been trying to live in the past.
   - ❑ "Driving the Wrong Way on a One-Way Street"—I need to turn m[y] life around.

Bible Study / 30 Minutes

Option 1 / Gospel Study

John 13:1–17 / Tough Act to Follow

This story occurs during a special meal Jesus ate with his disciples on the night before his death. It was customary for people's dusty, sandaled feet to be washed, usually by the lowest-ranking servant, before a meal was served. Have someone read John 13:1–17 and then discuss the questions with your group.

13 *It was just before the Passover Feast. Jesus knew that the time had come for him to leave this world and go to the Father. Having loved his own who were in the world, he now showed them the full extent of his love.*

²The evening meal was being served, and the devil had already prompted Judas Iscariot, son of Simon, to betray Jesus. ³Jesus knew that the Father had put all things under his power, and that he had come from God and was returning to God; ⁴so he got up from the meal, took off his outer clothing, and wrapped a towel around his waist. ⁵After that, he poured water into a basin and began to wash his disciples' feet, drying them with the towel that was wrapped around him.

⁶He came to Simon Peter, who said to him, "Lord, are you going to wash my feet?"

⁷Jesus replied, "You do not realize now what I am doing, but later you will understand."

⁸"No," said Peter, "you shall never wash my feet."

Jesus answered, "Unless I wash you, you have no part with me."

⁹"Then, Lord," Simon Peter replied, "not just my feet but my hands and my head as well!"

¹⁰Jesus answered, "A person who has had a bath needs only to wash his feet; his whole body is clean. And you are clean, though not every one of you." ¹¹For he knew who was going to betray him, and that was why he said not every one was clean.

¹²When he had finished washing their feet, he put on his clothes and returned to his place. "Do you understand what I have done for you?" he asked them. ¹³"You call me 'Teacher' and 'Lord,' and rightly so, for that is what I am. ¹⁴Now that I, your Lord and Teacher, have washed your feet, you also should wash one another's feet. ¹⁵I have set you an example that you should do as I have done for you. ¹⁶I tell you the truth, no servant is greater than his master, nor is a messenger greater than the one who sent him. ¹⁷Now that you know these things, you will be blessed if you do them."

1. Why do you think Jesus washed his disciples' feet?
   - ❐ to humble them
   - ❐ to show them an example of servanthood
   - ❐ because he loved them
   - ❐ because no task was beneath him

2. What would you have done if you had been there and Jesus approached you to wash your feet?
   - ❐ left the room
   - ❐ refused to let him
   - ❐ broken down and cried
   - ❐ felt honored by his caring act
   - ❐ just sat there—feeling guilty and unworthy
   - ❐ jumped up and tried to wash *his* feet

3. Who is one person in your life who has demonstrated what it means to "wash feet"? What did that person do for you?
   - ❐ my mother
   - ❐ my father
   - ❐ another family member
   - ❐ my spouse
   - ❐ a friend
   - ❐ someone I worked with
   - ❐ a teacher
   - ❐ a coach
   - ❐ a pastor
   - ❐ a small group leader
   - ❐ other:_____

4. What is the closest you have come to being part of a community that genuinely cared for one another and showed it?
   - ❐ a sports team
   - ❐ a music or drama group
   - ❐ a church
   - ❐ my family
   - ❐ the "gang" I used to run around with
   - ❐ a group of people I got to know at a retreat or camp
   - ❐ I'm not sure I have experienced this
   - ❐ a youth group
   - ❐ a mission trip I went on
   - ❐ a small group
   - ❐ other:_____

5. What do you do for others right now which is most like "washing feet"? How do you feel about doing this?

6. What would it mean to practice footwashing in your daily lifestyle—home? Work? Church?
   - ❐ to take care of others more
   - ❐ to let others take care of me
   - ❐ to do things that aren't "my job"
   - ❐ to show more affection or appreciation
   - ❐ to be more patient and forgiving
   - ❐ to serve with no strings attached
   - ❐ other:_____

Leadership Training Supplement

YOU ARE
HERE

BIRTH	GROWTH	RELEASE

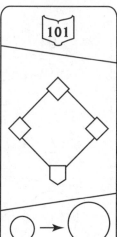
101

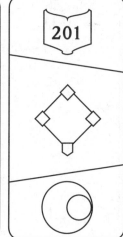
201

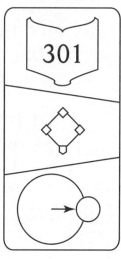
301

What is the game plan for your group in the 101 stage?

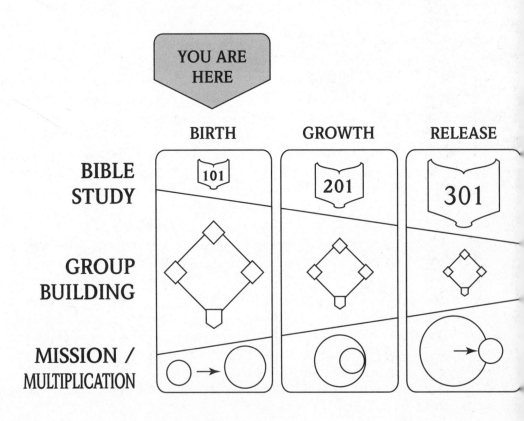

YOU ARE HERE

	BIRTH	GROWTH	RELEASE
BIBLE STUDY	101	201	301
GROUP BUILDING			
MISSION / MULTIPLICATION			

3-Legged Stool

The three essentials in a healthy small group are Bible Study, Group Building and Mission / Multiplication. You need all three to stay balanced—like a 3-legged stool.
- To focus only on Bible Study will lead to scholasticism.
- To focus only on Group Building will lead to narcissism.
- To focus only on Mission will lead to burnout.

You need a game plan for the life cycle of the group where all three of these elements are present in a mission-driven strategy. In the first stage of the group, here is the game plan:

Bible Study

To share your spiritual story through Scripture.

The greatest gift you can give a group is the gift of your spiritual story—the story of your spiritual beginnings, your spiritual growing pains, struggles, hopes and fears. The Bible Study is designed to help you tell your spiritual story to the group.

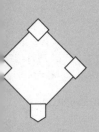

Group Building

To become a caring community.

In the first stage of a group, note how the baseball diamond is larger than the book and the circles. This is because Group Building is the priority in the first stage. Group Building is a four-step process to become a close-knit group. Using the baseball diamond illustration, the goal of Group Building—bonding—is home plate. But to get there you have to go around the bases.

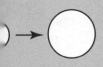

Mission / Multiplication

To grow your group numerically and spiritually.

The mission of your group is the greatest mission anyone can give their life to—to bring new people into a personal relationship with Christ and the fellowship of a Christian community. This purpose will become more prominent in the second and third stages of your group. In this stage, the goal is to invite new people into your group and try to double.

Bible Study

In the first stage of a group, the Bible Study is where you get t[]
know each other and share your spiritual stories. The Bible Stud[]
is designed to give the leader the option of going LIGHT c[]
HEAVY, depending on the background of the people in the group[]
OPTION 1 is especially designed for beginner groups who do n[]
know a lot about the Bible or each other. OPTION 2 is for group[]
who are familiar with the Bible and with one another.

Option 1

Relational Bible Study (Stories)

Designed around a guided questionnaire, the questions mov[]
across the Disclosure Scale from "no risk" questions about peo[]
ple in the Bible story to "high risk" questions about your own lif[]
and how you would react in that situation. "If you had been i[]
the story ..." or "The person in the story like me is ... " The ques[]
tions are open-ended—with multiple-choice options and n[]
right or wrong answers. A person with no background know[]
edge of the Bible may actually have the advantage because th[]
questions are based on first impressions.

The STORY   GUIDED QUESTIONNAIRE   My STOR[]
in Scripture   1   2   3   4   5   6   7   8   compare[]

OPTION 1: Light *RELATIONAL BIBLE STUDY*	*OPTION 2: Heavy* *INDUCTIVE BIBLE STUDY*
• Based on Bible stories • Open-ended questions • To share your spiritual story	• Based on Bible teachings • With observation questions • To dig into Scripture

Option 2

Inductive Bible Study (Teachings)

For groups who know each other, OPTION 2 gives you th[]
choice to go deeper in Bible Study, with questions about the te[]
on three levels:

- Observation: What is the text saying?
- Interpretation: What does it mean?
- Application: What are you going to do about it?

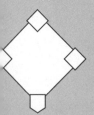

Group Building

The Baseball Diamond illustrates the four-step sharing process in bonding to become a group: (1) input; (2) feedback; (3) deeper input; and (4) deeper feedback. This process is carefully structured into the seven sessions of this course, as follows:

 Sharing My Story. My religious background. My early years and where I am right now in my spiritual journey.

 Affirming Each Other's Story. "Thank you for sharing ..." "Your story became a gift to me ..." "Your story helps me to understand where you are coming from ..."

 Sharing My Needs. "This is where I'm struggling and hurting. This is where I need to go—what I need to do."

 Caring for One Another. "How can we help you in prayer this week?" Ministry occurs as the group members serve one another through the Holy Spirit.

Mission / Multiplication

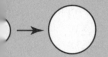

To prove that your group is "Mission-Driven," now is the time to start praying for your new "baby"—a new group to be born in the future. This is the MISSION of your group.

The birthing process begins by growing your group to about 10 or 12 people. Here are three suggestions to help your group stay focused on your Mission:

1. **Empty Chair.** Pull up an empty chair at the Caring Time and ask God to fill this chair at the next meeting.

2. **Refrigerator List.** Jot down the names of people you are going to invite and put this list on the refrigerator.

3. **New Member Home.** Move to the home of the newest member—where their friends will feel comfortable when they come to the group. On the next page, some of your questions about bringing new people into your group are answered.

Q&A

What if a new person joins the group in the third or fourth session?

Call the "Option Play" and go back to an OPTION 1 Bible Study that allows this person to "share their story" and get to know the people in the group.

What do you do when the group gets too large for sharing?

Take advantage of the three-part agenda and subdivide into groups of four for the Bible Study time. Count off around the group: "one, two, one, two"—and have the "ones" move quickly to another room for sharing.

What is the long-term expectation of the group for mission?

To grow the size of the group and eventually start a new group after one or two years.

What do you do when the group does not want to multiply?

This is the reason why this MISSION needs to be discussed at the beginning of a group—not at the end. If the group is committed to this MISSION at the outset, and works on this mission in stage one, they will be ready for multiplication at the end of the final stage.

What are the principles behind the Serendipity approach to Bible Study for a beginner group?

1. *Level the Playing Field.* Start the sharing with things that are easy to talk about and where everyone is equal—things that are instantly recallable—light, mischievously revealing and childlike. Meet at the human side before moving into spiritual things.

2. *Share Your Spiritual Story.* Group Building, especially for new groups, is essential. It is crucial for Bible Study in beginner groups to help the group become a community by giving everyone the opportunity to share their spiritual history.

3. *Open Questions / Right Brain.* Open-ended questions are better than closed questions. Open questions allow for options, observations and a variety of opinions in which no one is right or wrong. Similarly, "right-brained" questions are

better than "left-brained" questions. Right-brained questions seek out your first impressions, tone, motives and subjective feelings about the text. Right-brained questions work well with narratives. Multiple-choice questionnaires encourage people who know very little about the Bible. Given a set of multiple-choice options, a new believer is not threatened, and a shy person is not intimidated. Everyone has something to contribute.

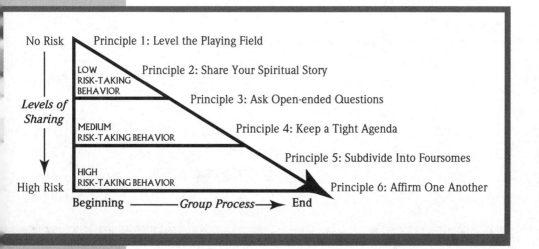

4. Tight Agenda. A tight agenda is better than a loose agenda for beginning small groups. Those people who might be nervous about "sharing" will find comfort knowing that the meeting agenda has been carefully organized. The more structure the first few meetings have the better, especially for a new group. Some people are afraid that a structured agenda will limit discussion. In fact, the opposite is true. The Serendipity agenda is designed to keep the discussion focused on what's important and to bring out genuine feelings, issues, and areas of need. If the goal is to move the group toward deeper relationships and a deeper experience of God, then a structured agenda is the best way to achieve that goal.

5. Fearless Foursomes. Dividing your small group into foursomes during the Bible Study can be a good idea. In groups of four, everyone will have an opportunity to participate and you can finish the Bible Study in 30 minutes. In groups of eight or more, the Bible Study will need to be longer and you will take away from the Caring Time.

Also, by subdividing into groups of four for the Bible Study time, you give others a chance to develop their skills at leading a group—in preparation for the day when you develop a small cell to eventually move out and birth a new group.

6. **Affirm the person and their story.** Give positive feedback to group members: "Thank you for sharing ... " "Your story really helps me to understand where you are coming from ... " "Your story was a real gift to me ... " This affirmation given honestly will create the atmosphere for deeper sharing.

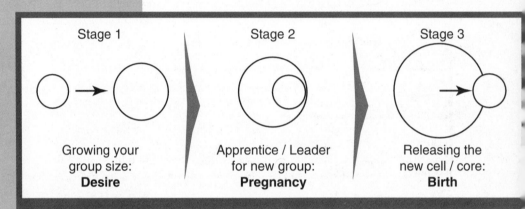

Stage 1	Stage 2	Stage 3
Growing your group size: **Desire**	Apprentice / Leader for new group: **Pregnancy**	Releasing the new cell / core: **Birth**

What is the next stage of our group all about?

In the next stage, the 201 BIBLE STUDY is deeper, GROUP BUILDING focuses on developing your gifts, and in the MISSION you will identify an Apprentice / Leader and two others within your group who will eventually become the leadership core of a new group down the road a bit.

7. In general, what's holding you back from living a lifestyle of service like Jesus demonstrated and taught?

   ❏ I'm afraid I'll be taken advantage of.

   ❏ I don't have time.

   ❏ I'm not willing to do menial tasks.

   ❏ I haven't had many good role models.

   ❏ I guess I'm too selfish.

   ❏ nothing really—I'm doing my best.

   ❏ other:_____

8. What would it take for this group to get into the footwashing business?

   ❏ more time than we have

   ❏ a deeper commitment that may take some time

   ❏ how do we get started?

   ❏ we need time to think about it.

   ❏ other:_____

Option 2 / Epistle Study

Galatians 5:13–26 / Fruit of the Spirit

As Christians, we owe much of our understanding of what it means to live a Christian lifestyle to the apostle Paul. This passage is one of many in which Paul exhorts believers how to live. Read Galatians 5:13–26 and discuss the questions which follow with your group.

[13]You, my brothers, were called to be free. But do not use your freedom to indulge the sinful nature; rather, serve one another in love. [14]The entire law is summed up in a single command: "Love your neighbor as yourself." [15]If you keep on biting and devouring each other, watch out or you will be destroyed by each other.

[16]So I say, live by the Spirit, and you will not gratify the desires of the sinful nature. [17]For the sinful nature desires what is contrary to the Spirit, and the Spirit what is contrary to the sinful nature. They are in conflict with each other, so that you do not do what you want. [18]But if you are led by the Spirit, you are not under law.

[19]The acts of the sinful nature are obvious: sexual immorality, impurity and debauchery; [20]idolatry and witchcraft; hatred, discord, jealousy, fits of rage, selfish ambition, dissensions, factions [21]and envy; drunkenness, orgies, and the like. I warn you, as I did before, that those who live like this will not inherit the kingdom of God.

[22]But the fruit of the Spirit is love, joy, peace, patience, kindness, goodness, faithfulness, [23]gentleness and self-control. Against such things there is no law. [24]Those who belong to Christ Jesus have crucified the sinful

Scripture continued on page 34

nature with its passions and desires. ²⁵Since we live by the Spirit, let *keep in step with the Spirit. ²⁶Let us not become conceited, provoking a* *envying each other.*

1. When you first moved away from home, what did "freedom" mean you? Free to do what? Free from what?

2. What does it mean to be "free" in Christ?

3. What does verse 13 say to those who think their freedom in Chr allows them to do anything they want?

4. Although we have been liberated from spiritual slavery, what kind servants do we become (vv. 13–15)? What grade would you get being this kind of servant?

5. As Paul indicates in verse 17, what two things are in conflict w each other?

6. How can you and God's Spirit defeat the sinful nature and grow fruit of the Spirit (see note on v. 24)?

7. Which of the acts of the sinful nature (vv. 19–21) are dead and bur in your life? Which are mortally wounded? Which are alive and we

8. Which of the fruit of the Spirit (vv. 22–23) are blossoming in your right now? Which are still in the bud?

9. What is the biggest change that being a Christian has made in yo lifestyle? How do you sense God calling you to change your lifesty

Caring Time / 15–45 Minutes

Take time to share any personal prayer requests. During your ti of prayer, remember those requests as well as needs that were sha during the Bible Study. If you're not sure how to begin, finish this s tence:

"Lord, I want to talk with you about my friend ..."

Don't forget to keep praying for the empty chair and inviting people your group.

Reference Notes

Summary. Paul founded the churches in Galatia during his first missionary journey. After leaving, apparently some Jewish Christians arrived. Accusing Paul of omitting parts of the Gospel, these false teachers said that the Galatians needed to submit to Jewish regulations in order to be truly Christian. This letter is a ringing declaration that salvation is God's free gift. After repeatedly warning his readers against losing their freedom by submitting to Jewish legalism, Paul now warns them about losing their freedom by submitting to sinful desires.

5:13 *free. But ...* What Paul has written about freedom from the Law could be misunderstood to be a license to indulge in all of one's appetites, and certainly he does not mean that. So he begins this new section on Christian living by examining the use of freedom. What Paul is calling for is responsible freedom, which, as he says, is the freedom to serve others in love.

freedom. Christian freedom stands between the extreme of legal bondage (life lived within a web of requirements) and the other extreme of unbridled indulgence (life lived without regard to any rules). Paul has already said that no one can be truly free until Christ takes away his or her burden of guilt (Christ frees a person from the power of the Law). Now he will show that one also needs to be freed from the power of sinful desires, which comes by the infilling of the Holy Spirit.

the sinful nature. The self-serving, self-seeking, self-indulgent aspect of human nature (see verses 19–21 for a partial list of its works).

serve. Literally, serve as slaves. The only form of slavery that is compatible with freedom is self-giving to others.

5:14 Paul echoes the teaching of Jesus in this summary of the Law (Mark 12:28–31).

5:16 *live by the Spirit.* Literally, walk by the Spirit, i.e., let the way you live, your conduct, be directed by the Holy Spirit. It is the Holy Spirit, not the Law, who will bring about a moral lifestyle.

5:17 Two principles are at war in the Christian's life. "But the believer is not the helpless battle ground of two opposing forces. If he yields to the flesh, he is enslaved by it, but if he obeys the prompting of the Spirit, he is liberated" (Bruce).

5:20 *idolatry.* The worship of any idol, be it a carved image of God (a statue) or an abstract substitute for God (a status symbol). An idol is identified as such because when faced with a choice, a person will follow its leading.

witchcraft. *Pharmakeia* is literally "the use of drugs," which was often associated with the practice of sorcery.

hatred. This is the underlying political, social and religious hostility whi... drives individuals and communities apart.

discord. This is the type of contention which leads to factions.

selfish ambition. This word came to refer to anyone who worked only f... his or her own good and not for the benefit of others.

factions. This means the party spirit which leads people to regard tho... with whom they disagree as enemies.

5:21 drunkenness. In the first century, diluted wine was drunk regula... by all ages, but drunkenness was not common and was condemn... (because it was thought to turn a person into a beast).

5:22–23 fruit of the Spirit. These traits characterize the child of God. T... list is representative; not exhaustive. LOVE: (*agape;*) the self-givir... active benevolence that is meant to characterize Christian love. JOY: T... Greek word is *chara*, and comes from the same root as "grace" (*charis*)... is not based on earthly things or human achievement; it is a gift from G... based on a right relationship with him. PEACE: The prime meaning of t... word is not negative ("an absence of conflict"), but positive ("the presen... of that which brings wholeness and well-being"). PATIENCE: This is t... ability to be steadfast with people, refusing to give up on them. KIN... NESS: This is the compassionate use of strength for the good of anoth... GOODNESS: This implies moral purity which reflects the character... God. FAITHFULNESS: This is to be reliable and trustworthy. GENTL... NESS: According to Aristotle, this is the virtue that lies between excess... proneness to anger and the inability to be angry; it implies control of or... self. SELF-CONTROL: This is control of one's sensual passions, ratf... than control of one's anger (as in gentleness).

5:23 there is no law. While it is possible to legislate certain forms... behavior, one cannot command love, joy, peace, etc. These are each g... of God's grace. With this list of qualities one moves into a whole new re... of reality, well beyond the sphere of Law.

5:24 have crucified the sinful nature. It is via the cross that a pers... dies to the power of the Law (2:19). Paul indicates here that in the sa... way, a person also dies to the power of their sinful nature. The verb ir... cates that this is not something done *to* the Christian but *by* the Christi... The Christian actively and deliberately has repented of (turned av... from) the old wayward patterns of life.

5:25 live by the Spirit. In the same way that the death of the ego (the... principle) is replaced by the mind of Christ (2:20), here Paul indicates ... the death of the sinful nature is replaced by the life of the Spirit.

SESSION

5

Money

3-PART AGENDA

ICE-BREAKER
15 Minutes

BIBLE STUDY
30 Minutes

CARING TIME
15–45 Minutes

Money—how to get it, how to use it and how to keep it—these pursuits probably consume more time and energy than any other human endeavor. We dream about having more; we worry about not having enough. As someone once said, "If money can't buy happiness, at least it can buy off unhappiness."

Although we may not like to admit it, the "American Dream" is primarily the pursuit of a better life through improving our economic position. Despite the fact that Americans have one of the highest standards of living in the world, we want more. But does more bring us happiness or bring us closer to God? When Mother Teresa was visiting the United States, she was asked to comment on her impressions of America. She stated that while India was mired in tremendous physical poverty, America experienced widespread spiritual poverty.

> **LEADER: If you haven't already, now is the time to start thinking about the next step for your group. Take a look at the 201 courses (the second stage in the small group life cycle) on the inside of the back cover.**

For some of us money means security. We may stash cash for those ominous rainy days or for a "safe" retirement. Others of us see money as a way of obtaining self-worth. After all, isn't money life's report card? We usually esteem people who have large amounts of money. We make them our leaders—in government, in business, and in the church. Still others sadly equate money with affection. Money and gifts may be given as a substitute for love or given with "strings attached."

Jesus understood the attraction of money and spoke about it often. In the following studies, we will see that while money is not inherently evil, it is often abused. As an alternative, Scripture teaches that money is a tool to be used to further God's kingdom. In the parable in the Option 1 Study, Jesus shows us the effects of greed. In the Option 2 Study (from 1 Timothy), the apostle Paul reiterates the dangers of money and exhorts those who are wealthy to be generous.

Ice-Breaker / 15 Minutes

Irresistible Bargains. Many of us find bargains hard to pass u▮ Go around and let each person answer the first question. Then go arour▮ on the second question.

1. Which of the following bargains would you have the greatest troub▮ resisting? Rank your top two.
   - ❒ 30% off sale on fine gourmet chocolates
   - ❒ one month of a premium cable channel free for signing up f▮ another month
   - ❒ "second entree free" coupon at a romantic restaurant
   - ❒ free airline ticket in exchange for looking at time-share property
   - ☑ 2-for-1 sale in the clothing department of my favorite store
   - ❒ box seats at general admission prices for my favorite sports tea▮
   - ❒ fine piece of antique furniture going for two-thirds of the list▮ value
   - ❒ chance to get tickets for live performance of my favorite singer▮ band for half-price
   - ❒ free membership to an athletic club or gym for a month

2. Rank where you would fall on the following continuum. "When▮ comes to bargains, I am generally ..."

1	2	3	4	5▮
cynical	suspicious	cautious	receptive	rea▮ and ea▮

Bible Study / 30 Minutes

Option 1 / Gospel Study

Luke 12:13–21 / Rich Fool

In the following story, Jesus warns us to "watch out" for the danger▮ placing top priority on the quest for material wealth. Have one pers▮ read Luke 12:13–21 out loud, and then discuss your responses to the▮ lowing questions with your group.

¹³Someone in the crowd said to him, "Teacher, tell my brother to div▮ the inheritance with me."

¹⁴Jesus replied, "Man, who appointed me a judge or an arbiter between you?" ¹⁵Then he said to them, "Watch out! Be on your guard against all kinds of greed; a man's life does not consist in the abundance of his possessions."

¹⁶And he told them this parable: "The ground of a certain rich man produced a good crop. ¹⁷He thought to himself, 'What shall I do? I have no place to store my crops.'

¹⁸"Then he said, 'This is what I'll do. I will tear down my barns and build bigger ones, and there I will store all my grain and my goods. ¹⁹And I'll say to myself, "You have plenty of good things laid up for many years. Take life easy; eat, drink and be merry." '

²⁰"But God said to him, 'You fool! This very night your life will be demanded from you. Then who will get what you have prepared for yourself?'

²¹"This is how it will be with anyone who stores up things for himself but is not rich toward God."

1. How would you describe the rich man in this parable?
   - ❐ a show-off
   - ❐ secure
   - ❐ materialistic
   - ❐ unhappy
   - ❐ brilliant
   - ❐ stupid
   - ❐ content
   - ❐ selfish

2. After he died, how would the local newspaper describe the rich man in their obituary?
   - ❐ a tireless worker
   - ❐ a success story
   - ❐ foolish
   - ❐ enterprising

3. How would you like to be remembered?
   - ❐ as a person who had a lot
   - ❐ as a person who gave a lot
   - ❐ as a person who built it all single-handedly
   - ❐ as a person who enjoyed what I had
   - ❐ as a person who sacrificed to be rich toward God

4. Why was God's reaction to the rich man so severe?
   - ❐ because God is intolerant of self-indulgent people
   - ❐ because God is jealous of all other "gods"
   - ❐ because God doesn't like rich people
   - ❐ because God has compassion for the poor

5. Which of the following is closest to how you view your money?
   - ❐ It's mine—keep your hands off!
   - ❐ It's God's—I just manage it.

39

6. What was your ambition in life when you were 18 years old?
  - ❐ I wanted to get a job and buy some things.
  - ❐ I wanted to go to college and have fun.
  - ❐ I wanted to go to college and get straight A's.
  - ❐ I wanted to get married and have a family.
  - ❐ I wanted to start a career.
  - ❐ I wanted to party all the time.
  - ❐ I wanted to make a million dollars by the time I was 30.
  - ❐ I had no ambition at all.
  - ❐ other:_____

7. Being totally honest, what is your greatest ambition now? (Choo the top three.)
  - ❐ getting a better job or advancing in my career
  - ❐ having nice things
  - ❐ having a good time
  - ❐ having a good marriage and family
  - ❐ having good friendships
  - ❐ having greater intimacy with God
  - ❐ making lots of money
  - ❐ making a contribution to the world
  - ❐ attaining financial independence
  - ❐ being true to myself
  - ❐ other:_____

8. How would you describe your primary financial goal at this point your life?
  - ❐ to earn enough money to pay my bills
  - ❐ to get out of debt
  - ❐ to set aside money for a secure retirement
  - ❐ to save money for_____
  - ❐ to make enough money to live like I really want to live
  - ❐ to give more money away than I am now
  - ❐ other:_____

9. How would it change the way you live if you took seriously Jes teaching that a "person's life does not consist in the abundance of possessions"?
  - ❐ I would probably have to join a monastery!
  - ❐ I would focus more on enjoying the free things in life.
  - ❐ I would be more generous with people in need.
  - ❐ I would give more to the church.
  - ❐ I wouldn't have such a big credit card bill.
  - ❐ I wouldn't change a thing—that's what I'm doing now.
  - ❐ other:_____

1 Timothy 6:3–10,17–19 / The Love of Money

In his letter to Timothy, his associate in ministry, the apostle Paul writes of the pros and cons of money. Read 1 Timothy 6:3–10,17–19 and discuss the questions which follow with your group.

³If anyone teaches false doctrines and does not agree to the sound instruction of our Lord Jesus Christ and to godly teaching, ⁴he is conceited and understands nothing. He has an unhealthy interest in controversies and quarrels about words that result in envy, strife, malicious talk, evil suspicions ⁵and constant friction between men of corrupt mind, who have been robbed of the truth and who think that godliness is a means to financial gain.

⁶But godliness with contentment is great gain. ⁷For we brought nothing into the world, and we can take nothing out of it. ⁸But if we have food and clothing, we will be content with that. ⁹People who want to get rich fall into temptation and a trap and into many foolish and harmful desires that plunge men into ruin and destruction. ¹⁰For the love of money is a root of all kinds of evil. Some people, eager for money, have wandered from the faith and pierced themselves with many griefs. ...

¹⁷Command those who are rich in this present world not to be arrogant nor to put their hope in wealth, which is so uncertain, but to put their hope in God, who richly provides us with everything for our enjoyment. ¹⁸Command them to do good, to be rich in good deeds, and to be generous and willing to share. ¹⁹In this way they will lay up treasure for themselves as a firm foundation for the coming age, so that they may take hold of the life that is truly life.

titude

1. What is one lesson or principle about money you can remember learning from your parents?

"I've never en a hearse pulling a U-haul!" —Charles Swindoll

2. What is the "great gain" in "godliness with contentment" (v. 6)?

3. What do you need financially or materially at this point in your life in order to be content?

4. What is dangerous about wanting to be rich (see especially vv. 9–10)? How do you think the desire for wealth could cause you to "fall into temptation and a trap"?

5. Is there a difference between enjoying money and being a lover of money (see vv. 10 and 17, and notes on v. 17)?

6. When in your life have you been the most tempted to become a "lov of money"?

7. What is Paul saying, particularly in verses 17–19, to people who ha plenty of money?

8. If you're really honest, what percentage of your hope is in wealth, a what percentage of your hope is in God?

9. What is your biggest concern about money right now?

"Give according to your income lest God make your income according to your giving."
—Peter Marshall

♥ Caring Time / 15–45 Minutes

Take a few minutes at the close to share any concerns and pr for one another. Answer this question:

"How can we help you in prayer this week?"

LEADER: Ask the group, "Who are you going to invite next week?"

Then, go around and let each person pray for the person on their rig Start with the sentence:

"Dear God, I want to speak to you about my friend _____

Reference Notes

Summary. In the context of this letter, Paul summarizes the problem false teachers and Timothy's role in dealing with them. In the process, provides some more details about the false teachers. It turns out t what motivates them is pride, a love of arguments, and greed (vv. 3– However, what really ought to motivate us, Paul says, is "godliness w contentment" (vv. 6–10).

6:3 *false doctrines.* Paul returns to the theme with which he began letter (1 Tim. 1:3). The false teachers have departed from the teaching Jesus (see also 1 Tim. 1:10; 4:6).

6:4 *unhealthy interest.* Literally, "being sick or diseased." This sor "morbid craving" (Bauer) stands in sharp contrast to the sound "healthy") instruction of verse 3.

6:5 *godliness is a means to financial gain.* As Paul has hinted in 3:3 and 8, the bottom line motivation of these false teachers is the money they make from their teaching. Paul does not consider it wrong for a person to be paid for teaching (see 5:17–18), but he is incensed when greed is the main motivation for ministry.

6:6–10 Paul picks up on this problem of greed and says two things about it. First, godliness is to be much preferred to profit (vv. 6–8), and second, a love of money brings dire results (vv. 9–10).

6:6 This verse stands in immediate contrast to the last words in verse 5, with a striking play on terms. They think godliness "is a way to become rich." Well (in Greek, *de*, meaning "indeed"), they are right. There *is* great profit (now used metaphorically) in godliness (religion does make a person very rich), provided it is accompanied by a "contented spirit" (Moffatt, Kelly); that is, if one is satisfied with what one has and does not seek material gain (Fee).

contentment. This was a favorite word of the Stoic philosophers from whom Paul borrowed it. (Zeno, the founder of this philosophical school, came from Tarsus, Paul's hometown.) This word refers to a person who is not impacted by circumstances. Such a person is self-contained and thus able to rise above all conditions. For Paul, however, this sort of contentment was derived from the Lord (see Phil. 4:11).

6:7–8 There are two reasons why "godliness" with contentment" brings great gain. First, at death people can take nothing with them: So why worry about material gain that has to be given up in the end any way? Second, if people have the essentials in life, this should be enough.

6:9–10 Paul ends by pointing out the dangers of riches. In these verses, he chronicles the downward process that begins with the desire "to get rich." Such a desire leads into "temptation," which is, in turn, "a trap." The "trap" is the "many foolish and harmful desires" that afflict the greedy person The end result is that such people are "plunge(d) into ruin and destruction."

6:9 *temptation.* Greed causes people to notice and desire what they might not otherwise have paid attention to.

6:10 *For the love of money is a root of all kinds of evil.* Paul is probably quoting a well-known proverb in order to support the assertion he makes in verse 9 that the desire for money leads to ruin. This verse is often misquoted as "money is the root of all evil." While Paul clearly sees the danger of money, he is not contending that *all* evil can be traced to avarice.

Some people ... have wandered. Here is the problem. Some of the false teachers have given in to the temptation to riches. They were probably once good leaders in the church but they got caught by Satan (1 Tim. 4:1–2), became enamored with speculative ideas (6:3–5), and in the end were pulled down by their love for money.

6:17–19 The preceding doxology with its exalted language in praise of God would have provided a fine ending to this letter. But Paul realized that he must say a few more words about riches, lest he be misunderstood. In verses 9–10, he said some very strong things about money. His concern there was with the false teachers and their use of "godliness [as] a means to financial gain" (v. 5). However, what about those who were already rich? To them Paul says: "Do not place your ultimate trust in your wealth. It is part of this world that is passing away. Place your trust in God and be generous in sharing your wealth."

6:17 ***those who are rich.*** This is the only place in his letters that Paul addresses the wealthy directly. His consistent "command" is that the rich share their wealth with the poor (see also Rom. 12:8,13; 2 Cor. 9:6–15). "The whole teaching of the Christian ethic is not that wealth is a sin, but that wealth is a very great responsibility" (Barclay).

not to be arrogant nor to put their hope in wealth. These are the two dangers of wealth—that it will cause people to think themselves to be better than others, and that they might put their trust in their riches (and not in God).

for our enjoyment. But Paul is no ascetic. That the wealthy should not place confidence in their wealth does not carry with it an attitude of total rejection. God, he says, "richly provides us with everything for our enjoyment" (see also 1 Tim. 4:3–4; Eccl. 5:19–20). *Enjoyment*, however, does not mean self-indulgent living (1 Tim. 5:6). The reason *everything* may be enjoyed lies in the recognition that everything, including one's wealth, a *gift,* the expression of God's gracious generosity (Fee).

6:18 In this verse Paul tells the rich in four different ways to share their wealth.

Career

3-PART AGENDA

ICE-BREAKER
15 Minutes

BIBLE STUDY
30 Minutes

CARING TIME
15–45 Minutes

If you find yourself in any social setting where you are meeting new people, most likely one of the first questions you will be asked is "Where do you work?" or "What do you do for a living?" In our culture, a significant amount of our identity is connected to what we do vocationally. Unless we have consciously chosen not to work outside our home, we all want a career or job which pays us well, allows us flexibility, and fulfills us as individuals.

But many of us find that our jobs don't fulfill those desires. In this session, we will take an assessment of our work lives. Is the thrill of your career gone? Is it a major battle just to roll out of bed in the morning? Has that job which you once considered so exciting and challenging become drudgery? Do you find yourself thinking about doing something else?

Changing careers, and even just changing jobs, can be a traumatic experience. While you may fantasize about starting your own business or pursuing a life-long interest, a career change may hold its own disappointments. What you may really need is an attitude adjustment! For others, for a variety of reasons, a career change may be a necessity.

> **LEADER: This is the next to last session in this course. At the end of the course, how would you like to celebrate your time together? With a dinner? With a party? With a commitment to continue as a group?**

As with our time and money, our career really is a gift from God. The word *vocation* has its origin in the sense of a "calling." The key to assessing your job or career is to reflect on God's calling for your life. In the context of your relationship with this group, you will have an opportunity to do that in this session.

The passage in Option 1 is a parable Jesus told about some workers who felt, quite understandably, that they were treated unfairly. In the Option 2 Study (from Paul's letter to the Romans), we will consider our outlook toward our career—and specifically toward using our spiritual gifts.

Ice-Breaker / 15 Minutes

Dream Career. What would you do if you could choose an career? Look at the list below and choose two: your first choice and yo last choice. If you have time, let other group members take turns gues ing what you have selected.

POLICE OFFICER: A brave upholder of the law in an exciting fig against criminals.

ENTERTAINER: You can sing, dance and act. The darling of Hollywoo and Vegas.

HIGH-POWERED ATTORNEY: An eloquent, intelligent representative the law who defends the innocent in the courtroom.

PRESIDENT OF THE U.S.: The buck stops here. Leader of the fre world.

FASHION MODEL: Drop dead gorgeous. The walking definition of glam

TEACHER: An educator who inspires students to expand their horizo and appreciate the world.

SURGEON: Saving lives is just another day at work. Is there a Doctor the house?

MISSIONARY: The bold preacher who is willing to go around the world share the Gospel.

PSYCHOLOGIST: The trusted counselor who helps people come peace with themselves.

ASTRONAUT: A daring outer space pilot and extraterrestrial scientist.

MINISTER: A beloved servant who takes care of a congregation's sp tual needs.

RACE CAR DRIVER: A courageous competitor who tears around track at 200 mph.

VETERINARIAN: The beloved animal doctor everyone trusts with th pets and livestock.

NOVELIST: The fiction writer who can produce best-sellers that everyo talks about.

YOUR PICK: _____

Bible Study / 30 Minutes

Option 1 / Gospel Study

Matthew 20:1–16 / Attitudes at Work

This is a parable Jesus told about workers in a vineyard. Landowners had full-time servants who took care of the daily needs of the estate; but in busy times, such as at harvest, they would hire day laborers to help with the work that the regular servants couldn't do on their own. At these times, men would gather in the village and hope that they might be hired. Read Matthew 20:1–16 and discuss the questions with your group.

20 *"For the kingdom of heaven is like a landowner who went out early in the morning to hire men to work in his vineyard. ²He agreed to pay them a denarius for the day and sent them into his vineyard.*

³"About the third hour he went out and saw others standing in the marketplace doing nothing. ⁴He told them, 'You also go and work in my vineyard, and I will pay you whatever is right.' ⁵So they went.

"He went out again about the sixth hour and the ninth hour and did the same thing. ⁶About the eleventh hour he went out and found still others standing around. He asked them, 'Why have you been standing here all day long doing nothing?'

⁷"'Because no one has hired us,' they answered.

"He said to them, 'You also go and work in my vineyard.'

⁸"When evening came, the owner of the vineyard said to his foreman, 'Call the workers and pay them their wages, beginning with the last ones hired and going on to the first.'

⁹"The workers who were hired about the eleventh hour came and each received a denarius. ¹⁰So when those came who were hired first, they expected to receive more. But each one of them also received a denarius. ¹¹When they received it, they began to grumble against the landowner. ¹²'These men who were hired last worked only one hour,' they said, 'and you have made them equal to us who have borne the burden of the work and the heat of the day.'

¹³"But he answered one of them, 'Friend, I am not being unfair to you. Didn't you agree to work for a denarius? ¹⁴Take your pay and go. I want to give the man who was hired last the same as I gave you. ¹⁵Don't I have the right to do what I want with my own money? Or are you envious because I am generous?'

¹⁶"So the last will be first, and the first will be last."

1. If you were one of the first workers hired (at 6 a.m.), how would you react at the end of the story?
   ❑ I would never work for that jerk again!
   ❑ I would report the landowner to the Better Business Bureau.
   ❑ I would grumble behind the landowner's back.
   ❑ I wouldn't complain, because I got the pay I agreed to.
   ❑ I would be happy for the workers who got hired after I did.

2. From an employer's viewpoint, how would you react to the landowner's wage practices?
   ❑ He was too soft-hearted.
   ❑ He was unfair to the first workers.
   ❑ He was right—he could do what he wanted with his money.
   ❑ He was a compassionate man.
   ❑ He didn't have a business mind.

3. What was your first job? How did you choose your career path, and how fairly do you feel you have been compensated?

4. What is the main reason you work?
   ❑ to survive
   ❑ to give our children a better life
   ❑ to obtain money and material things
   ❑ to be able to give some of my earnings
   ❑ because work is fulfilling
   ❑ because I would be bored otherwise
   ❑ because I feel called to
   ❑ other: _____

5. How would you evaluate your career outlook on the following scale?

   I LOOK UPON MY CAREER AS:

Just a job to endure							A high calling from God
1	2	3	4	5	6	7	8 9

   I DEMONSTRATE THE ATTITUDE THAT:

I am my own boss							God is my "boss"
1	2	3	4	5	6	7	8 9

6. What do you consider the biggest drawback about your work?
   ❑ an excessive workload or long hours   ❑ irritating coworkers
   ❑ an unreasonable boss   ❑ poor pay / benefits
   ❑ monotonous or meaningless work   ❑ job insecurity
   ❑ balancing work with the rest of life   ❑ other: _____
   ❑ the toll work takes on my family

7. How would you describe your attitude toward work right now?
   ❐ It's a paycheck.
   ❐ It's drudgery.
   ❐ I'm not really into it—I'm not giving it my all.
   ❐ I'm giving it my all—but I'm not getting much out of it.
   ❐ I'm giving it my all, and find some satisfaction in what I'm doing.
   ❐ I'm very fulfilled by my work.
   ❐ other:_____

8. What change might help the way you feel about work?
   ❐ to stop looking at work in terms of money only
   ❐ to stop looking at those in authority as my enemy
   ❐ to look at what I can contribute rather than what I can receive
   ❐ to look for ways God can use me in my job
   ❐ to try to use my gifts in my job more
   ❐ to focus on the people I work with and how God can touch them
      through me
   ❐ The only change that would help would be a change of jobs.
   ❐ other:_____

9. Comparing your energy level and attitude about your career to this
   parable, what "time" is it in your life right now?
   ❐ 6 a.m.—I'm raring to go.
   ❐ 9 a.m.—I'm feeling productive.
   ❐ Noon—I'm ready for a break.
   ❐ 3 p.m.—I'm running out of gas.
   ❐ 5 p.m.—Help, I *am* out of gas!
   ❐ 6 p.m.—I'm enjoying looking back at what I have accomplished.

Option 2 / Epistle Study

Romans 12:1–8 / Using Your Gifts

The first 11 chapters of the apostle Paul's letter to the Romans are known
for their emphasis on doctrine and theology. With chapter 12, Paul shifts
to practical teaching for how believers should live. Paul writes that one of
the ways we can please God and strengthen the body of Christ is by
knowing and using our spiritual gifts. Read Romans 12:1–8 and discuss
the following questions with your group.

12 *Therefore, I urge you, brothers, in view of God's mercy, to offer you bodies as living sacrifices, holy and pleasing to God—this is you spiritual act of worship. ²Do not conform any longer to the pattern of th world, but be transformed by the renewing of your mind. Then you will able to test and approve what God's will is—his good, pleasing and perfe will.*

³For by the grace given me I say to every one of you: Do not think yourself more highly than you ought, but rather think of yourself with sob judgment, in accordance with the measure of faith God has given you. ⁴Ju as each of us has one body with many members, and these members not all have the same function, ⁵so in Christ we who are many form o body, and each member belongs to all the others. ⁶We have different gif according to the grace given us. If a man's gift is prophesying, let him u it in proportion to his faith. ⁷If it is serving, let him serve; if it is teaching, him teach; ⁸if it is encouraging, let him encourage; if it is contributing to t needs of others, let him give generously; if it is leadership, let him gove diligently; if it is showing mercy, let him do it cheerfully.

1. As a teen, how much did peer pressure affect you?

2. What does it mean to you to "offer your body as a living sacrifice" God (v. 1)?

3. How do you "renew" your mind (v. 2)? What is the result of doing s

4. When it comes to career planning and advancement, what are sor common "patterns of this world" (v. 2)?

5. How much influence has your Christian faith and values had up your career planning?

6. Being really honest, are you more inclined to "think of yourself mc highly than you ought" (v. 3) or to put yourself down?

7. Which of the spiritual gifts listed in verses 6–8 matches you be Which of these gifts do you see in the others in this group?

PROPHET / PERCEIVER: Truth-oriented. Forthright, outspok uncompromising. Open to inspired messages from God, and cal to pray about what is perceived.

SERVER: Needs-oriented. Practical, hard-working, conscientious satisfied when things get done, regardless of who gets the credit.

"God has not called me to be successful; he has called me to be faithful."
—Mother Teresa

50

TEACHER: Concept-oriented. Systematic. Logical. Has good insight into Scripture and makes things clear to others.

ENCOURAGER / EXHORTER: Growth-oriented. Good at setting goals and motivating others. Disciplined and single-minded.

GIVER: Cause-oriented. Loves to give. Able to see "big picture" and assess resources. Handles money wisely.

LEADER / ADMINISTRATOR: Task-oriented. Organized, decisive, thrives under pressure. Good at delegating responsibility and getting things done through others.

MERCY / COMPASSION PERSON: Feeling-oriented. Highly sensitive to others in need. Good at listening, affirming, caring and "being present" when someone is hurting.

8. To what extent are you using the special gifts God has given you in your life in general, and in your career in particular?

9. How could you use your gifts, especially in your career, more fully than you do?

COMMENT

Paul also talked about the gifts given to Christians in his first letter to the Corinthians:

12 Now about spiritual gifts, brothers, I do not want you to be ignorant. ²You know that when you were pagans, somehow or other you were influenced and led astray to mute idols. ³Therefore I tell you that no one who is speaking by the Spirit of God says, "Jesus be cursed," and no one can say, "Jesus is Lord," except by the Holy Spirit.

⁴There are different kinds of gifts, but the same Spirit. ⁵There are different kinds of service, but the same Lord. ⁶There are different kinds of working, but the same God works all of them in all men.

⁷Now to each one the manifestation of the Spirit is given for the common good. ⁸To one there is given through the Spirit the message of wisdom, to another the message of knowledge by means of the same Spirit, ⁹to another faith by the same Spirit, to another gifts of healing by that one Spirit, ¹⁰to another miraculous powers, to another prophecy, to another distinguishing between spirits, to another speaking in different kinds of tongues, and to still another the interpretation of tongues. ¹¹All these are the work of one and the same Spirit, and he gives them to each one, just as he determines.

1 Corinthians 12:1–11

Caring Time / 15–45 Minutes

Give everyone a chance to answer the question:

"How can we help you in prayer this week?"

Go around and let each person pray for the person on their right.

Reference Notes

Summary. From doctrine Paul now turns almost by reflex to duty: how one lives flows quite naturally out of what one believes. Exposition has become exhortation.

12:1 *in view of God's mercy.* A Christian's motivation to obedience overwhelming gratitude for God's mercy.

bodies. The Christian lifestyle is not a matter of mystical spirituality that transcends one's bodily nature, but an everyday, practical exercise love (Rom. 6:13; 13:8). The idea of "bodies" also emphasizes the metaphor of sacrifice since one puts bodies on the altar.

sacrifices. In the Old Testament sacrificial system, the victim of the sacrifice becomes wholly the property of God. Sacrifice becomes holy, i.e. set apart for God only.

living ... holy ... pleasing to God. In Greek, these three phrases are attached with equal weight as qualifiers to "sacrifices." The idea is not that God counts living sacrifices the same as the dead animals in the old system, but rather that he wants Christians to live in fullness of life, accord with his principles (i.e., sanctification), and hence to be the kind sacrifice desired by God.

spiritual act of worship. Paul may mean by this an inner movement the part of a person toward God (in contrast to external rites). But since the word translated "spiritual" can be rendered "rational," the idea may that believers render intelligent worship. This meaning is given credence by the emphasis in verse 2.

12:2 *Do not conform.* Believers are no longer helpless victims of natural and supernatural forces which would shape them into a distorted pattern; rather they now have the ability to resist such powers.

be transformed. The force of the verb is "continue to let yourself be transformed"; i.e., a continuous action by the Holy Spirit which goes on for a lifetime. A Christian's responsibility is to stay open to this process as the Spirit works to teach them to look at life from God's view of reality.

renewing of your mind. Develop a spiritual sensitivity and perception—learn to look at life on the basis of God's view of reality. Paul emphasizes the need to develop understanding of God's ways.

test and approve. Christians are called to a responsible freedom of choice and action, based on the inner renewing work of the Holy Spirit.

12:3–8 Paul now turns to the Christian community as a whole—understanding it to be composed of believers with different gifts.

12:3 ***every one of you.*** The truth about spiritual gifts applies to each believer.

sober judgment. The command is to know oneself (especially one's gifts) accurately, rather than to have too high an opinion of oneself in comparison to others. This attitude enables a body of believers to blend their gifts together in harmonious ministry.

measure of faith. Believers are not to measure themselves against others, but against the standard God has given them. Thus they can achieve a true estimate of themselves.

12:4–5 Using a picture that could be understood in all cultures—the body—Paul defines the nature of the Christian community: diverse gifts, but all part of one body, the body of Christ.

12:5 ***each member belongs to all the others.*** This is the critical insight that makes for harmony in the church. Believers must recognize that they are interdependent, needing to give to and receive from one another.

12:6 ***gifts.*** Those endowments given by God to every believer by grace (the words "grace" and "gifts" come from the same root word) to be used in God's service. The gifts listed here (or elsewhere) are not meant to be exhaustive or absolute since no gift list overlaps completely.

prophesying. Inspired utterances, distinguished from teaching by their immediacy and unpremeditated nature, the source of which is direct revelation by God. Prophesying was highly valued in the New Testament church (1 Cor. 14:1).

in proportion to his faith. This could mean that prophets are to resist adding their own words to the prophecy, or it could mean that they must measure their utterances in accord with "the faith"; i.e., Christian doctrine.

12:7 *serving.* The capacity for rendering practical service to the needy

teaching. In contrast to the prophet (whose utterances have as the source the direct revelation of God), the teacher relied on the Ol Testament Scriptures and the teachings of Jesus to instruct others.

12:8 Paul concludes his brief discussion of spiritual gifts with this emphasis on the fact that whatever gift one has, it should be exercised wit enthusiasm for the good of others!

encouraging. This is supporting and assisting others to live a life of obdience to God.

contributing. The person who takes delight in giving away his or h possessions.

leadership. Those with special ability to guide a congregation are calle upon to do so with zeal.

mercy. "The person whose special function is, on behalf of the congr gation, to tend the sick, relieve the pain, or care for the aged or disable (Cranfield). Note that three of the seven gifts involve practical assistan to the needy.

P.S.
If the next session is your last session together, you may want to plar party to celebrate your time together. Save a few minutes at the close this session to make these plans.

SESSION

7

Future

3-PART AGENDA

ICE-BREAKER
15 Minutes

BIBLE STUDY
30 Minutes

CARING TIME
15–45 Minutes

In a way we have come full circle in this course on personal assessment. We began by evaluating our goals and priorities. We were then challenged to apply those convictions in the areas of time, lifestyle, money and career. In this last session, we will consider our goals and priorities as they relate to an assessment of our future.

Dreams about our future make life exciting and worthwhile. They help us go beyond present reality. Dreams are different than fantasies. Fantasies are merely wishes which we have no thought of ever realizing. But dreams are what we hope will come true one day. Sometimes as we age, we give up our dreams and life becomes routine and unexciting. James Michener wrote in *The Drifters,* "The permanent defeat of life comes when dreams are surrendered to reality."

> **LEADER: Read the bottom part of page M8 in the center section concerning future mission possibilities for your group. Save plenty of time for the evaluation and future planning during the Caring Time. You will need to be prepared to lead this important discussion.**

Of course the only way we can realize our dreams is to take risks. A small minority of people thrive on taking risks. They live by the principle that the only real failure is the failure to try. But taking risks doesn't come easy for most of us. In the Option 1 Study, we will have a chance to identify with a story about Peter—when he was confronted with an opportunity to take a risk that for most of us would be threatening.

The flip side of taking healthy risks is trusting our future completely to God. Jesus advocated both sides of this equation. In the Parable of the Talents he commended the two servants who took some risks to invest in the kingdom, and denounced the other servant who played it safe and hid his talent in the ground. And in the passage in the Option 2 Study (from the Sermon on the Mount), Jesus instructed his followers to trust God rather than to worry about their lives now or in the future.

Ice-Breaker / 15 Minutes

Automotive Affirmation. Use this list of automotive items affirm the contribution of each person in your group. Have someone rea out loud the first item—BATTERY. Then, let everyone in the group call o the name of the person in your group who best fits this description.

BATTERY: A dependable "die-hard"—provides the "juice" for everythin to happen.

SPARK PLUG: Gets things started. Makes sure there is "fire," even c cold mornings.

OIL: "The razor's edge" to protect against engine wear-out, provid longer mileage, and reduce friction for fast-moving parts.

SHOCK ABSORBER: Cushions heavy bumps. Makes for an easy, cor fortable ride.

RADIO: The "music machine," making the trip fun and enjoyable. Adds little "rock 'n' roll" for a good time.

MUFFLER: Reduces the engine's roar to a cat's "purr," even at hi speeds over rough terrain.

CUP HOLDER: The servant, always meeting a need.

TIRE JACK: Bears the burdens of others. Is a strong support in time need.

TRANSMISSION: Converts the energy into motion, enables the engine slip from one speed to another without stripping the gears.

SEAT BELT / AIR BAG: Restrains or protects others when there is a pc sibility of them getting hurt.

GASOLINE: Liquid fuel that is consumed, giving away its own life for t energy to keep things moving .

WINDSHIELD: Keeps the vision clear, protects from flying objects.

Bible Study / 30 Minutes

Matthew 14:22–33 / Walking on Water

Everyone can identify with Peter. He seemed to have a knack for saying or doing the wrong thing. But he also was someone who was willing to take risks. Have someone read this story from Matthew 14:22–33 out loud, and then discuss the questions with your group.

22Immediately Jesus made the disciples get into the boat and go on ahead of him to the other side, while he dismissed the crowd. 23After he had dismissed them, he went up on a mountainside by himself to pray. When evening came, he was there alone, 24but the boat was already a considerable distance from land, buffeted by the waves because the wind was against it.

25During the fourth watch of the night Jesus went out to them, walking on the lake. 26When the disciples saw him walking on the lake, they were terrified. "It's a ghost," they said, and cried out in fear.

27But Jesus immediately said to them: "Take courage! It is I. Don't be afraid."

28"Lord, if it's you," Peter replied, "tell me to come out on the water."

29"Come," he said.

Then Peter got down out of the boat, walked on the water and came toward Jesus. 30But when he saw the wind, he was afraid and, beginning to sink, cried out, "Lord, save me!"

31Immediately Jesus reached out his hand and caught him. "You of little faith," he said, "why did you doubt?"

32And when they climbed into the boat, the wind died down. 33Then whose who were in the boat worshiped him, saying, "Truly you are the Son of God."

1. If you had been with the disciples and saw someone walking on the water, what would you have said?
  ❏ "I'm seeing things!"
  ❏ "Where's Jesus?!"
  ❏ "Let me out of here!"
  ❏ "Do you see what I see?"
  ❏ "I think I ate too many anchovies."
  ❏ I would have been speechless.

2. What do you learn about Peter from this story?
   ❒ He was crazy.
   ❒ He was a risk-taker.
   ❒ He had the most faith of all the disciples.
   ❒ He was impulsive.
   ❒ He had good intentions.

3. What made Peter sink?
   ❒ His sandals got waterlogged.
   ❒ He lost confidence in himself.
   ❒ His focus shifted from Jesus to his circumstances.
   ❒ His fear was greater than his faith.
   ❒ He realized how foolish he had been to step out of the boat.

4. How are you at "stepping out of the boat" and taking risks?
   ❒ daring
   ❒ cautious—I put my big toe in first.
   ❒ just plain scared
   ❒ I'll try anything once.
   ❒ I'm good at going second.

5. What dreams do you have for your future? What risks are involved?

6. What is the relationship between risk-taking and faith?
   ❒ There is no relationship.
   ❒ It's okay to be a risk-taker if you have faith in Christ.
   ❒ Risk-taking is good if you have faith in yourself.
   ❒ A life of faith is a life of risk-taking.

7. Where do you specifically feel that God is inviting you to get out of the boat right now?
   ❒ in my job / career—trying something risky
   ❒ in my relationships—dealing with a problem
   ❒ in my inner life—facing a hang-up
   ❒ in my future planning—doing something I've been afraid to try
   ❒ in my spiritual walk—putting God first
   ❒ other:_____

8. What do you think might make you "sink"?
   ❒ fear of failure   ❒ fear of standing alone
   ❒ inconsistency   ❒ spiritual or intellectual doubt
   ❒ unhealthy relationships   ❒ other:_____
   ❒ a sense of inadequacy
   ❒ an impulse to rush into things before counting the cost

9. What would be the best way for God to help you?
❏ be very gentle with me
❏ assure me it's okay to fail
❏ give me a push
❏ give me a lot of support people
❏ get out of the boat with me

Option 2 / Gospel Study

Matthew 6:25–34 / Not to Worry

Immediately preceding this passage, Jesus had stated, "You cannot serve both God and Money." The implication of this principle is that the disciple need not worry about the necessities of life (specifically, food, drink and clothing). By way of illustrating the fact that God takes care of those who follow him, Jesus notes that birds depend upon God for their food, and flowers depend on him for their beautiful adornment. His point is that God's children, who are more valuable than the birds and the flowers, can therefore depend upon God to show the same care for them that he gives to birds and plants. To worry is to show a lack of dependence on God.

In the following passage from the Sermon on the Mount, Jesus points out the proper focus we should have about our future. These words probably had even more relevance when Jesus spoke them. Having enough food and clothing to survive was much more uncertain in those days than it is in most countries today. Read Matthew 6:25–34 and then discuss the questions as a group.

[25]"Therefore I tell you, do not worry about your life, what you will eat or drink; or about your body, what you will wear. Is not life more important than food, and the body more important than clothes? [26]Look at the birds of the air; they do not sow or reap or store away in barns, and yet your heavenly Father feeds them. Are you not much more valuable than they? [27]Who of you by worrying can add a single hour to his life?

[28]"And why do you worry about clothes? See how the lilies of the field grow. They do not labor or spin. [29]Yet I tell you that not even Solomon in all his splendor was dressed like one of these. [30]If that is how God clothes the grass of the field, which is here today and tomorrow is thrown into the fire, will he not much more clothe you, O you of little faith? [31]So do not worry, saying, 'What shall we eat?' or 'What shall we drink?' or 'What shall we wear?' For the pagans run after all these things, and your heavenly Father knows that you need them. [33]But seek first his kingdom and his righteous-

Scripture continued on page 60

59

ness, and all these things will be given to you as well. [34]Therefore do no worry about tomorrow, for tomorrow will worry about itself. Each day ha enough trouble of its own.

1. Who is the worrier in your family? Who is calm and collected even i the hardest of times?

2. According to Jesus, why does worrying about your needs and you future show a lack of faith in God? What does the illustration of God care for the birds and lilies teach you? *En owp grace of God*
don't trust
more valuable

3. What does it mean to "seek first his kingdom and his righteou ness"—and how is this a solution for worrying (see note on v. 33)?
mind in different places Choice
Choosing forget precious

4. Are God's children exempt from hunger, famine and other suffering If we're not promised trouble-free days (v. 34), what *are* we promise (see notes on v. 34)?

○ Call to be God's servant

5. By saying "do not worry about tomorrow" (v. 34), what does Jes mean?
   ❑ Don't plan ahead.
   ❑ Plan ahead so you don't worry.
   ❑ Live for today.
   ❑ God will take care of you no matter what you do.
   ■ Trust God with things you can't control.

6. Other Scriptures call on people to plan ahead, work hard, and pr vide for their families (Prov. 6:6–8; 10:4; 2 Thess. 3:6–12). How c you reconcile those admonitions with Jesus' statements here?

7. How do you feel about your long-range plans for providing for yc children, preparing for retirement, etc.?

8. What concerns you most about the future? How much do you wo about that? How much do you pray about it?

9. Where do you need God's guidance in your plans for the future?

Caring Time / 15–45 Minutes

EVALUATION

1. Take some time to evaluate the life of your group by using the statements below. Read the first sentence out loud and ask everyone to explain where they would put a dot between the two extremes. When you are finished, go back and give your group an overall grade in the categories of Group Building, Bible Study and Mission.

GROUP BUILDING

On celebrating life and having fun together, we were more like a ...
wet blanket _____hot tub

On becoming a caring community, we were more like a ...
prickly porcupine _____cuddly teddy bear

BIBLE STUDY

On sharing our spiritual stories, we were more like a ...
shallow pond _____spring-fed lake

On digging into Scripture, we were more like a ...
slow-moving snail _____voracious anteater

MISSION

On inviting new people into our group, we were more like a ...
barbed-wire fence _____wide-open door

On stretching our vision for mission, we were more like an ...
ostrich _____eagle

2. What are some specific areas in which you have grown in this course on personal assessment? *— Important piece of group Evaluate*
❏ learning how to open up and share my life with others
❏ having a closer relationship with God
❏ setting new and improved personal priorities
❏ discovering how to better use my time
❏ developing a lifestyle of service and faithfulness
❏ acquiring a healthier perspective about money
❏ desiring to have the right attitude about my work or career
❏ trusting God for my future and the risks I need to take
❏ other:_____

• understand scripture
listening to others

61

MAKE A COVENANT

A covenant is a promise made to each other in the presence of God. I[t] purpose is to indicate your intention to make yourselves available to o[ne] another for the fulfillment of the purposes you share in common. In a sp[ir]it of prayer, work your way through the following sentences, trying [to] reach an agreement on each statement pertaining to your ongoing li[fe] together. Write out your covenant like a contract, stating your purpos[e,] goals and the ground rules for your group.

1. The purpose of our group will be ... (finish the sentence)

2. Our goals will be ...

3. We will meet for _____weeks, after which we will decide if we wi[sh] to continue as a group.

4. We will meet from _____ to _____ and we will strive to start on tim[e] and end on time.

5. We will meet at _____ (place) or we will rota[te] from house to house.

6. We will agree to the following ground rules for our group (check):

   ❏ PRIORITY: While you are in the course, you give the group mee[t]ings priority.

   ❏ PARTICIPATION: Everyone participates and no one dominates.

   ❏ RESPECT: Everyone is given the right to their own opinion, and questions are encouraged and respected.

   ❏ CONFIDENTIALITY: Anything that is said in the meeting is nev[er] repeated outside the meeting.

   ❏ EMPTY CHAIR: The group stays open to new people at eve[ry] meeting, as long as they understand the ground rules.

   ❏ SUPPORT: Permission is given to call upon each other in time [of] need at any time.

   ❏ ACCOUNTABILITY: We agree to let the members of the gro[up] hold us accountable to the commitments which each of us make[in] whatever loving ways we decide upon.

   ❏ MISSION: We will do everything in our power to start a new gro[up.]

   outreach —

6:25 *Therefore I tell you.* This passage spells out the significance of the principles Jesus laid down in Matthew 6:19–24. Since disciples of Jesus have a heavenly treasure (6:20), and their loyalty is to God and not Money; *therefore*, they need not be anxious about the material needs of life.

do not worry. Worry or anxiety is a state of mind. Having chosen God's way, the disciple must not be overly concerned about the demands and pressures that occupy those committed to the other way (materialism).

is not life more important than food ...? The materialistic quest reduces life to a matter of keeping the body fed and dressed. While that is a necessary part of life, the materialistic answer makes this the central focus.

6:26 In showing the folly of making concern for food the central focus of life, Jesus points out how God provides for the needs of the birds. The point is not that his disciples need not do anything to feed themselves, but that their ultimate trust rests in God to meet their needs. "What is prohibited is worry, not work" (France).

much more valuable. The point of the creation story (Gen. 1) is to stress God as creator of all and the role of humanity as God's representative on earth, charged with the responsibility to "rule" the earth (such that it is nurtured and prosperous). It is because humanity has a special relationship and responsibility to the Creator that people are "more valuable" than animals. Since God meets the needs of the animals, will he not do so for people? This does not mean that Christians are somehow exempt from the possibility of hunger or famine. The common sufferings of humanity affect believers, too.

6:27 *a single hour.* Jesus' point is that since all the worry in the world cannot even add an hour to one's life, what is the purpose of worrying? (Modern medicine might add that worry actually will probably reduce one's life span through stress-related diseases!) While the older versions of the Bible rendered this "a single cubit," this translation makes more sense in this context. Even if worry *could* add a single hour to one's entire life, that would not be a very significant payoff for all the anxiety. However, if worry could actually add a cubit (about 18 inches) to one's height, that would be a major accomplishment.

6:28–30 Following through on his comment in verse 25, Jesus now encourages his followers to consider how even flowers, unable to rush about in anxious pursuit of their physical needs, are adorned with beauty. Since God provides them with such beauty, why should his people fear that they will be neglected by God?

6:29 *Solomon.* Solomon, the third king of Israel, was noted for his fabulous wealth (1 Kings 10:14–29). The folly of being anxious about clothes is revealed in that even the simplest flower is adorned more delicately and attractively than the richest man or woman.

6:30 *thrown into the fire.* Some of the flowers Jesus has in mind are not the ornamental ones most often noticed for their beauty. Even weeds that were commonly used for fuel have a beauty that far surpasses their intended use. Therefore, people can have the assurance God will not forget to provide them with needed clothes.

you of little faith. This is a single Greek word meaning "little-faiths." Matthew uses it four of the five times it appears in the New Testament (8:26; 14:31; 16:8; 17:20). As the two illustrations here show, faith reliance on the love, care and power of God. Faith is the opposite anxiety.

6:31 *So do not worry.* Again, what is commended here is not idleness but faith. As verse 33 indicates, the disciples of Jesus are to be busy, but their activity is centered around pursuing God's agenda; they are not be centered around simply meeting their own needs. They are to be confident that God will meet their needs.

"What shall we eat / drink / wear?" This is the "world's Trinity of care" (Stott).

6:33 Having described where their attention is *not* to be directed (toward worry), Jesus now tells his disciples where their focus *is* meant to be. They are to be oriented toward God's unfolding work ("his kingdom") and on acts that reflect his nature ("his righteousness"). All of one's life—from one's inner attitudes to one's social involvements—is to be brought under this overriding purpose. The supreme ambition of the Christian is that that he or she thinks, says, and does be for the glory of God. The implication of this verse is that if a disciple is focused on finding and doing the will of God, then that disciple will not worry about material things. His her needs are in the hands of God.

6:34 *tomorrow.* Worry generally has to do with the future, about what lies ahead. The disciple is to live one day at a time, and not in dread of what might happen in the future.

trouble. Disciples are not promised a trouble-free life; they are, however, promised God's care.